EQUIPPED FOR BATTLE

WEAPONS, GEAR, AND UNIFORMS OF AMERICA'S WARS

AMERICAN REVOLUTION • CIVIL WAR • WWI • WWII • VIETNAM WAR • IRAQ WAR

EQUIPPED FOR BATTLE

WEAPONS, GEAR, AND UNIFORMS OF AMERICA'S WARS

AMERICAN REVOLUTION · CIVIL WAR · WWI · WWII · VIETNAM WAR · IRAQ WAR

by Michael Burgan, Eric Fein, and Shelley Tougas

CAPSTONE PRESS
a capstone imprint

Published by Capstone Press,
1710 Roe Crest Drive, North Mankato, Minnesota 56003.
www.capstonepub.com

Library of Congress Cataloging-in-Publication Data
Burgan, Michael.
Equipped for battle : weapons, gear, and uniforms of America's wars : American Revolution, Civil War, WWI, WWII, Vietnam War, Iraq War /
by Michael Burgan, Eric Fein, Shelley Tougas.
pages cm
Summary: "Describes weapons, gear, and uniforms used by various military forces during America's biggest wars"—Provided by publisher.
Includes index.
ISBN 978-1-4765-7653-4 (pbk.)
1. United States—Armed Forces—Weapons systems—History—Juvenile literature. 2. Military weapons—United States—History—Juvenile
literature. 3. United States—Armed Forces—Uniforms—History—Juvenile literature. 4. Military uniforms—United States—History—Juvenile
literature. I. Fein, Eric. II. Tougas, Shelley. III. Title.
UF503.B87 2014
623.40973—dc23   2013029631

Summary: "Describes weapons, gear, and uniforms used by various military forces during America's biggest wars."—Provided by publisher.

Editorial Credits
Aaron Sautter, editor; Ted Williams, designer; Eric Manske, production specialist

Photo Credits
Alamy: akg-images, 70 (top), 83 (bottom), Classic Image, 13 (left), 41 (top), 43 (right), Dorling Kindersley, 77 (bottom), INTERFOTO, 24
(bottom), 70 (bottom), 78 (top); AP Images: 98 (top), 127, 129 (left), 133 (bottom), Bilal Hussein, 155 (bottom), Nick Ut, 130-131; Corbis: 81
(top), 83 (top), 99 (both), 100 (top), Bettmann, 44, 57 (bottom), 58, 73 (top), 74 (top), 85 (top), 88 (bottom), 120-121, 136 (top), Bettmann/Kyoichi
Sawada, 129 (right), 138 (bottom), Bettmann/Mathew B. Brady, 43 (left), Bettmann/V. McColley, 142 (top), Dazo Vintage Stock Photos/Images.
com, 69 (left), DK Limited/Gary Ombler, 136 (bottom), Hulton-Deutsch Collection, 64-65, 68, 71 (bottom), 74 (bottom), 82, 86, 87 (bottom), 98
(bottom), Medford Historical Society Collection/Andrew J. Russell, 54 (bottom), Nik Wheeler, 137 (bottom), PoodlesRock, 32, Tim Page, 137 (top),
144; CorbisRF, 55 (bottom); Corel, 105 (bottom); DoD photo 164 (bottom), Spc. Michael J. MacLeod, U.S. Army, 173; Dreamstime: Rose-marie
Henriksson, 31 (top); Gamma-Keystone via Getty Images/Keystone-France, 97 (top); Getty Images: AFP/STF, 92-93, AFP/Patrick Baz, 148-149,
Archive Photos, 114 (top), Archive Photos/George Eastman House, 85 (middle), Archive Photos/U.S Air Force photo, 143 (top), Buyenlarge,
47 (bottom), 59 (bottom), Dorling Kindersley/Gary Ombler, 100 (bottom), 101 (top), Fotosearch, 57 (top), 72, 84, 89, 115
(bottom), Hulton Archive/Express Newspapers, 134, 138 (top), Hulton Archive/FPG, 107 (top), Hulton Archive/Galerie Bilderwelt, 97 (bottom), 111
(bottom), Hulton Archive/Keystone, 115 (top), 116 (left), Hulton Archive/Three Lions, 85 (bottom), Hulton Archive/Topical Press Agency, 87 (top),
Imagno, 71 (top), Mansell/Time Life Pictures, 88 (top), Michael Ochs Archives, 109 (bottom), MPI, 59 (top), Photoquest, 60, Popperfoto, 96, 107
(bottom), Roger Viollet, 112 (bottom), 114 (bottom), Time Life Pictures/David E. Scherman, 108 (bottom), Time Life Pictures/Mansell, 110, Time
Life Pictures/Margaret Bourke-White, 101 (bottom); iStockphoto: Charles Knox, 54 (top), Craig DeBourbon, 171 (top), back cover, (bottom), Getty
Images/MPI/Hulton Archive, 34, 36-37; James P. Rowan, 27 (both), 28 (both), 29, 48 (top), 49 (bottom), 51 (bottom), 52 (top), 55 (middle),
61 (bottom), 106 (bottom), 112 (top), 113 (top); Ketchum Hand Grenade WICR 30377 in the collection of Wilson's Creek National Battlefield, 53
(top); Landov, 126, 140, The Plain Dealer/Brain Albrecht, 145; NARA, 62, 90, 117 (bottom); Newscom: AFP/Getty Images/Ahmad Al-Rubaye,
157 (top), 159, AFP/Getty Images/USMC/First Bat. Fifth Marines, 158, AFP/Karim Sahib, 155 (top), akg-images, 81 (bottom), 111 (top), 125,
128, 135 (top), C3622 Carl Schulze Deutsch Presse Agentur, 161 (middle), Central News/Mirrorpix, 75, Jose Luis Cuesta Digital Press Photos, 154,
KRT/Sylwia Kapuscinski, 163 (top), Official Photograph of the Australia Commonwealth/Mirrorpix, 73 (bottom), Photoshot/War/UPPA, 116
(right), SIPA/Berges Yves Guy, 124; Painting by Don Troiani/www.historicalimagebank.com, 8-9, 12, 13 (right), 14, 15 (top), 17, 40, 41 (bottom), 42;
Shutterstock: Adrian Grosu, 106 (top), BESTWEB, 78 (bottom), 77 (middle), Dennis Donohue, 26, Digital Media Pro, cover (flag), Gary Blakelev,
102 (bottom), Jackson Gee, 132, Michaela Stejskalova, 103 (top), Olemac, 102 (top), 103 (bottom), 106 (middle), back cover (left), Zagibalov
Aleksandr, 153, zimand, 163 (bottom); Super Stock Inc.: Science and Society, 61 (top), 69 (right); The National Guard Image Gallery Painting by
Domenick D'Andrea, 6, 19 (bottom); U.S. Air Force photo, 117 (top), 168 (both), SRA Greg L. Davis, 169 (bottom), Staff Sgt. Dallas Edwards, 165;
U.S. Army photo, 118, 135 (bottom), 139 (bottom), 142 (bottom), back cover (right), Frank Trevino, 167 (top), Lance Cpl. Michael J. Yellowhorse,
172, Sgt. Jason Stewart, 157 (bottom), Sgt. Justin Howe, 171 (bottom), Spc. Jared Eastman, 170 (top), Spc. 4 Long, 141, Spc. Teddy Wade, cover
(soldier), Staff Sgt. James Selesnick, 156, Staff Sgt. Michael L. Casteel, 146, 152; U.S. Marine Corps photo, 105 (top), Gunnery Sgt Mark Olivia,
164 (top); U.S. Navy photo, 143 (bottom), 167 (bottom), MC1 Eileen Kelly Fors, 166, MC2 Michael Russell, 169 (top); www.historicalimagebank.
com, 15 (bottom), 16 (both), 18, 19 (top), 20, 21 (top), 22, 23 (both), 24 (top), 25 (both), 30 (both), 31 (bottom), 45 (both), 46 (both), 47 (top), 48 (top), 49 (top), 52 (bottom), Connecticut Museum of History, 53 (bottom), 80 (top), West Point
Museum, 56, 76, 79 (bottom), 80 (bottom); Wikimedia, 79 (top), 109 (top), 139 (top), Antique Military Rifles, 77 (top), 104 (bottom), Dkamm, 104
(top), German Federal Archive/Esselborn, 113 (bottom), German Federal Archive/Toni Schneiders, 108 (top), M62, 161 (top), National War College
Military Image Collection, 170 (bottom), PEOSoldier, 160 (both), 161 (bottom), szuppo, 133 (top); Wikipedia: 162, Hmaag, 50 (both), 51 (top)

Artistic Effects
iStockphoto: Leslie Banks; Shutterstock: Anan Kaewkhammul, caesart, Donald Gargano, Eky Studio, Ewa Walicka, ever, Gary Paul Lewis,
Gwoeii, hektor2, Jules_Kitano, maigi, Oleg Golovnev, osov, Peter Cox, polispoliviou, Supertrooper, Susan Law Cain

Printed in the United States of America in Stevens Point, Wisconsin.
072013   007635R

TABLE OF CONTENTS

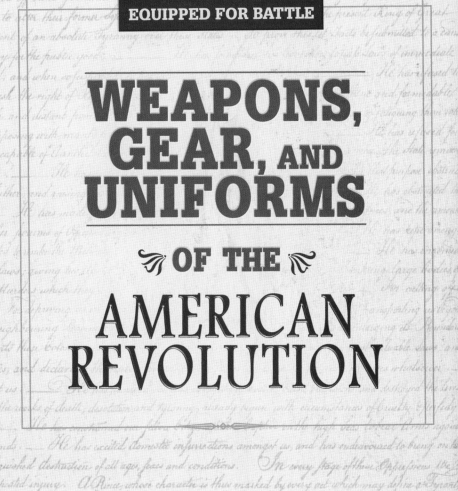

WEAPONS, GEAR, AND UNIFORMS

❧ OF THE ❧

AMERICAN REVOLUTION

THE AMERICAN REVOLUTION

On April 18, 1775, British troops marched out of Boston, Massachusetts, to seize the local militia's weapons and equipment. However, the colonists were prepared to defend their rights. With guns ready, the militia in Lexington waited for the Redcoats. When the two sides confronted each other, tempers flared. Without warning, shots were fired—and several colonists fell dead. The killings were just the first of the American Revolution.

The clash between the colonists and Great Britain had begun in 1764. The British government began raising taxes on its 13 American colonies. But no colonists sat in the British Parliament. The Americans had no say in making the tax laws that affected their lives. Many colonists became angry about taxes they felt were unfair.

In 1773 the British government passed the Tea Act. This law strengthened Britain's taxes on tea brought to the colonies. To protest the law, a group of colonists dumped thousands of pounds of tea into Boston Harbor. The Boston Tea Party angered the British, and Parliament passed new laws restricting freedoms in Massachusetts and the other colonies. Finally in 1775, the fighting in Lexington spurred the colonies to fight for independence from Britain.

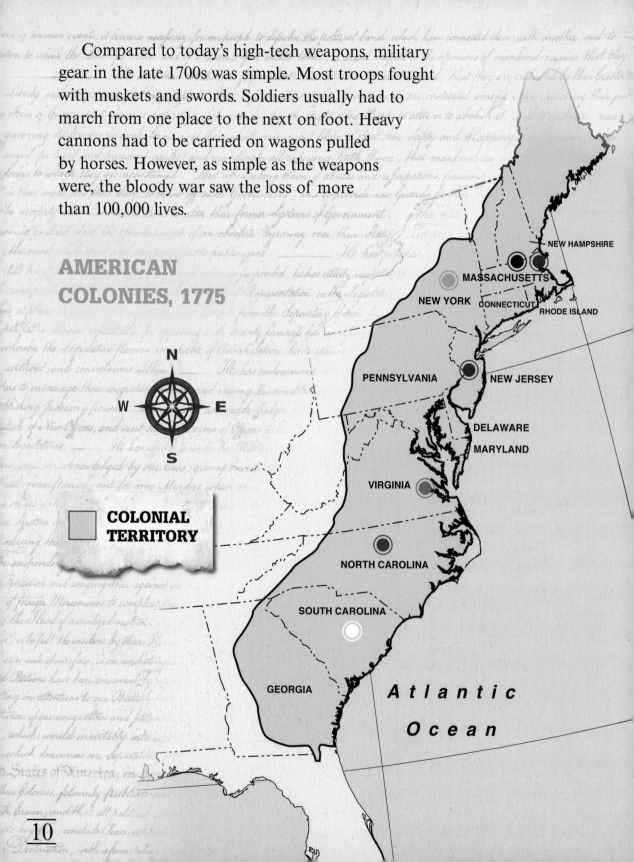

Compared to today's high-tech weapons, military gear in the late 1700s was simple. Most troops fought with muskets and swords. Soldiers usually had to march from one place to the next on foot. Heavy cannons had to be carried on wagons pulled by horses. However, as simple as the weapons were, the bloody war saw the loss of more than 100,000 lives.

AMERICAN COLONIES, 1775

NEW HAMPSHIRE

MASSACHUSETTS

NEW YORK   **CONNECTICUT**

RHODE ISLAND

PENNSYLVANIA   **NEW JERSEY**

DELAWARE

MARYLAND

VIRGINIA

COLONIAL TERRITORY

NORTH CAROLINA

SOUTH CAROLINA

GEORGIA

Atlantic Ocean

MAJOR AMERICAN REVOLUTION BATTLES

Lexington and Concord, Massachusetts
Fought: April 19, 1775
American casualties: 95
British casualties: 273

Camden, South Carolina
Fought: August 16, 1780
American casualties: 1,900
British casualties: 313

Bunker Hill, Charlestown, Massachusetts
Fought: June 17, 1775
American casualties: 441
British casualties: 1,054

Guilford Courthouse, North Carolina
Fought: March 15, 1781
American casualties: 420
British casualties: 532

Trenton, New Jersey
Fought: December 26, 1776
American casualties: 12
British casualties: 1,024

Yorktown, Virginia
Fought: October 6–19, 1781
American casualties: 252
British casualties: 635

Saratoga, New York
Fought: October 7, 1777
American casualties: 319
British casualties: 600

BATTLE FACT
During the war, privately owned U.S. ships called privateers captured or destroyed about 600 British ships.

AMERICAN UNIFORMS

American soldiers wore a variety of clothing. Militia men and others who could not afford uniforms wore their own clothes. For those who did have uniforms, the clothing depended on a soldier's rank and specific job. Basic uniforms included a shirt, jacket, and short pants known as breeches.

CONTINENTAL SOLDIERS
The main American fighting force was the Continental Army. Early in the war, soldiers wore long brown coats. But by 1779 most wore blue. U.S. marines wore green jackets.

HATS
Many soldiers wore a three-sided tricorn hat. Others wore cocked hats, with one part of the hat pinned up. Soldiers turned their cocked hats so the flat side faced their shooting arms. Wearing a hat this way made sure it wasn't in the way when the soldier fired his gun.

SAILORS
For daily ship life and battles at sea, sailors preferred loose, casual clothing.

FRONTIER SOLDIERS

Soldiers from the frontier usually wore hunting shirts. These were made of linen cloth. They were loose fitting so men could easily move their arms to fire.

CAVALRY HELMETS

American cavalry soldiers wore helmets to protect their heads if they fell from their horses. Some of the helmets had dyed horsehair attached to the top for decoration.

CONTINENTAL OFFICERS

Uniforms for officers varied. Officers' hats often included a decoration called a cockade. This small knot of colored ribbons helped show an officer's rank. Shoulder markings called epaulettes also showed an officer's rank.

BRITISH UNIFORMS

British soldiers were professionals. They were expected to wear their uniforms a certain way and look their best. But their colorful, fancy uniforms weren't always practical on the battlefield. Stiff shirt collars made it hard for soldiers to turn their heads, for example. Still, certain items of clothing were useful, such as helmets and straps for holding gear.

HATS

Some British troops wore tricorn hats. Others wore a leather infantry cap with a leather visor. Grenadier soldiers wore tall, heavy bearskin hats.

COATS

British soldiers were often called "Redcoats" because of their long red jackets. The bright color made it easy for the soldiers to see each other on the battlefield. However, the red color made it easier for American soldiers to see them too.

BRITISH CAVALRY

The arrival of British cavalry marked the first time these mounted troops were used in North America. British riders often wore metal helmets.

BATTLE FACT

One group of British cavalry wore brass helmets. A white skull was painted on the front, which stood for death. The words "or glory" were underneath it.

OFFICERS' GORGETS

An officer's formal uniform included a gorget. These small decorations were originally large metal breastplates that soldiers wore for protection in battle. But by the American Revolution, officers mainly wore them as symbols of their rank. They no longer offered much protection in battle. Some American officers, such as George Washington, also wore gorgets.

GEAR FOR DAILY LIFE

Both British and American troops carried most of the gear they needed. British soldiers received supplies from the government. But American troops often had trouble getting the supplies they needed. Continental soldiers often had to make their own gear. They also captured necessary supplies from the British.

HAVERSACKS

A cloth bag called a haversack held food and items a soldier needed to eat. Larger bags were called knapsacks and had two straps, one for each shoulder.

CANTEENS

Many soldiers carried their water in wooden canteens. A few canteens were made of metal. Larger wooden kegs were sometimes carried as well.

CANTEEN. CARRIED IN WAR 1776, REVOLUTION'S BY THE CONTINENTAL LINE NEW JERSEY

TINDERBOX

Starting a fire outdoors was important for cooking food and keeping warm. Soldiers kept fire-starting tools in a tinderbox. It contained a flint and steel that were struck together to create a spark. The box also held small strips of cloth that caught the spark and began to burn.

BEDROLLS

Bedrolls were worn over the shoulder. The simple bedding consisted of a ground cloth and a blanket. Soldiers slept with the ground cloth under them and covered themselves with the blanket.

KNIVES

Many soldiers carried a knife for eating, a pocketknife, and a fascine knife. Fascine knives had hooked blades that were useful for cutting small tree branches.

BATTLE FACT

Fascine refers to bundles of wood tied together. Soldiers placed these bundles of wood around cannons to provide some protection for the gunners.

TOOLS FOR WAR

Marching and fighting in the war was tiring. In addition to their weapons, soldiers had to carry several tools on the battlefield. Many tools were needed to prepare and fire the soldiers' muskets. Officers had tools to keep watch over a battle. Special equipment was also used to inspire soldiers to keep fighting as the battle raged on.

CARTRIDGES

Cartridges consisted of paper wrapped around metal balls, called shot, and gunpowder. A soldier usually bit open the top of the cartridge and poured some gunpowder into the musket's pan near the trigger. The rest of the gunpowder and the shot was then poured down the gun barrel. The soldier rammed down the shot and powder with a metal rod before firing the weapon.

POWDER HORNS

Some soldiers kept their shot and gunpowder separate. The powder was stored in hollow horns taken from a cow or other animal. The horns often had designs, pictures, or even maps carved into them.

BULLET MOLDS

Between battles, soldiers often needed to make their own shot. They carried ball-shaped molds made of stone or iron for this job. They poured molten lead into the molds to make bullets.

SPYGLASSES

Some officers carried small telescopes called spyglasses. These devices helped them watch enemy movements from far away.

DRUMS

Armies of the 1700s usually marched with musicians. Drums were used to send signals to troops on the battlefield. A type of flute called a fife was used to inspire soldiers as they marched and fought.

COLORS

Each group of soldiers had its own flag, or colors. The color bearer was a soldier who carried the raised flag into battle. The flag showed a unit's position on the battlefield.

LONG-BARREL GUNS

Before the American Revolution, guns were heavy and hard to reload. Newer flintlock muskets were an improvement, but were still hard to load and shoot. The best guns were rifles. Twisting grooves called rifling were cut inside the barrel. Rifling made the shot spin as it was fired, which helped the bullet fly straighter and farther.

MUZZLE-LOADING MUSKETS

Muzzle-loading muskets were the most common weapon of the war. The shot was loaded in the open end, or muzzle, of the gun barrel. The typical musket was more than 4 feet (1.2 m) long and weighed 8 to 12 pounds (3.6 to 5.4 kg).

FLINTLOCKS

Most guns at the time used a flintlock, which created a spark that fired the shot. Most soldiers could fire a flintlock musket three or four times a minute.

BATTLE FACT

The British musket was called the "Brown Bess" because of its brown, wooden stock. The name Bess might come from the German word busche, which means "bush."

CARBINES

Cavalry soldiers often used carbines. A carbine was shorter than a regular musket and fired slightly smaller shot. The carbine's lighter weight made it easier to carry and fire on horseback.

BREECH-LOADING RIFLES

British officer Patrick Ferguson perfected one of the world's first breech-loading rifles. Few were used during the war, perhaps because the British government did not realize how effective they were. Soldiers could fire faster when loading from the breech instead of the muzzle.

PENNSYLVANIA LONG RIFLES

Some American frontiersmen had guns called Pennsylvania long rifles. A good shooter could hit a target up to 200 yards (183 m) away with a Pennsylvania rifle. Common muskets were accurate only to about 50 yards (46 m). But the Pennsylvania was very slow to reload. For that reason, it was not very effective in battle.

PISTOLS AND GRENADES

In addition to long-barreled guns, soldiers used several smaller weapons. Pistols fired accurately, but only at short distances. Grenades were small explosives that could be thrown or sometimes fired from special guns.

CAVALRY PISTOLS

Cavalry troops often kept two pistols strapped to their saddles. Officers carried them too, though the average foot soldier did not. The guns stayed in leather pouches called holsters until needed.

POCKET PISTOLS

Some officers carried smaller guns called pocket pistols. These were easily hidden in an officer's pocket. One American version of this gun was just 7.5 inches (19 cm) long.

PISTOLS AT SEA

Sailors usually hung their pistols on a hook on their belts. The guns were handy when boarding an enemy ship or for defending their own ship. The barrels of these handguns were made of brass, which resisted the damaging effect of seawater.

BLUNDERBUSS

Some sailors and marines used a blunderbuss. This short musket had a wide barrel end. The blunderbuss sprayed small shot over a wide area. It was an effective weapon against enemies on a crowded ship's deck.

BATTLE FACT

The name for the blunderbuss came from the Dutch word *donderbus*, which means "thunder gun."

HAND GRENADES

A rarer small weapon was the hand grenade. A small, spherical iron container was filled with gunpowder. A soldier lit a fuse and then threw the grenade. When the lit fuse reached the powder, the grenade exploded.

SWORDS AND KNIVES

Thousands of years ago, people learned to create weapons from iron and steel. The metal allowed weapons to have both a cutting edge and a piercing point. During the American Revolution, both American and British soldiers used a variety of swords, knives, and other bladed weapons on the battlefield.

BAYONETS

A bayonet was one of a soldier's most important weapons. Most battles ended with enemies fighting in hand-to-hand combat. The bayonet turned a gun into a deadly spear with a long reach.

HUNTING SWORDS

Infantry troops carried straight swords. Some of these weapons were simple hunting swords used to kill an animal after it had been wounded.

CAVALRY SABERS

Cavalry soldiers favored swords called sabers. These slightly curved swords were ideal for soldiers on horseback when attacking enemy infantry troops.

LONG KNIVES

Soldiers also carried knives for a variety of uses. Riflemen often used long knives for hand-to-hand combat.

CUTLASSES

At sea, sailors used short swords called cutlasses. These smaller swords were ideal for close fighting on cramped ships.

TOMAHAWKS

On the frontier, small axes called tomahawks were used for cutting wood. But on the battlefield, tomahawks were deadly weapons. A soldier could fight off several enemies very quickly with a tomahawk. Soldiers could also use tomahawks as thrown weapons.

ARTILLERY

Large guns came in different sizes and had different uses. Artillery guns were named according to the weight of the shot they fired. At the start of the war, Americans had few artillery pieces. Many of the large guns used by Americans were captured from the British during the war.

FIELD CANNON

The basic field cannon had a long metal barrel. It fired a cannonball on a fairly straight path over long distances. Sometimes the cannonball was fired so it would bounce along the ground to wipe out advancing enemy troops.

18-POUNDER SIEGE GUN

Heavier cannons, such as 18-pounders, were often used during sieges of enemy locations. The heavy guns usually stayed in one spot. Soldiers used them to fire large shells at targets.

GRASSHOPPERS

The British had both 1.5- and 3-pound (0.7- and 1.4-kg) cannons that were sometimes called grasshoppers. The guns got this name because they tended to hop backward when fired.

SWIVEL GUN

The swivel gun was a small cannon. It was usually mounted on the side of a ship or the wall of a fort. Its barrel moved from side to side. Because of its small size, only two men were needed to load and fire it.

BATTLE FACT

Most artillery guns required up to five men to load, fire, and clean out the barrels between shots.

SPECIAL-USE ARTILLERY

Field guns were not useful in all situations. Some cannons could not be angled high enough to fire over an army's own troops. Military engineers came up with new designs that solved some of the limits of basic cannons.

MORTARS

Mortars had shorter and wider barrels than cannons. They were designed to fire shot or explosives at high angles over walls, trees, and friendly troops.

HOWITZERS

Howitzers had the best features of both cannons and mortars. They could fire at high angles like mortars. And they could fire at low angles like cannons. Howitzers could fire either solid shot or explosive shells.

NAVAL CANNONS

The carriages of naval cannons had small wheels. The guns only had to move short distances to be loaded and fired. The common 32-pounder weighed 5,500 pounds (2,495 kg).

CARRONADES

During the war the British developed a new naval cannon called a carronade. It was much lighter than most cannons, and it used less gunpowder. Nicknamed the "Smasher," a carronade could fire 68-pound (31-kg) shot.

COEHORNS

Some ships also carried coehorns. These small mortars were designed to be easily carried and fired.

FIRING THE BIG GUNS

Soldiers had to stand clear as they fired large artillery guns. The force of the shot could send the heavy gun and its carriage rolling back several feet. Unlike most ground troops, artillery gunners could fire several kinds of projectiles, depending on the targets.

CANNONBALL

Solid iron cannonballs could blast through the sides of wooden ships or buildings. Just one of these heavy balls could take out several enemy soldiers.

GRAPESHOT AND CANISTER

Canisters held many small iron balls called grapeshot. The balls spread out over a wide area after they were fired. They could hit several enemy troops at once.

EXPLOSIVE SHELL

Explosives were also used as projectiles. Gunners lit the fuse of an iron ball filled with gunpowder. The shell exploded over enemy troops. Those who weren't killed were showered with bits of hot metal.

CARCASS

A carcass was a shot covered or filled with flammable material that was lit before it was fired. Carcasses were usually used to set wooden buildings on fire.

CHAIN SHOT

Chain shot was sometimes used on ships. It cut through an enemy ship's ropes and sails.

WARFARE ON THE WATER

At the start of the war, the British and American navies were very different. The Americans had merchant ships but no real warships. The British had battleships with as many as 70 guns and 500 sailors. Captains often didn't like sinking enemy ships unless it was necessary. They simply wanted to capture the other vessel and anything useful it had on board.

SHIPS OF THE LINE

These were the largest fighting ships of the day. They could have up to three decks and as many as 120 guns. The heavier guns were placed on the lowest deck, with lighter guns on the upper decks.

UNDERWATER OBSTACLES

Americans used dangerous underwater obstacles to try to block British ships from sailing up rivers. One such obstacle was the spiked timber crib. Wooden timbers created a small pen that held large rocks. The rocks held up a large spike that could pierce the bottom of an enemy ship.

FLOATING BATTERIES

The floating battery was not really a ship. It looked more like a small fort that floated on a raft and held guns. Sailors would usually row them into place, but a few also used sails.

UNDERWATER MINES

Underwater mines were deadly explosive devices. A mine could blast a hole in a ship's hull, sinking it and removing it from battle.

BATTLE FACT

American David Bushnell built the *Turtle*, the first submarine. It was made to attach mines to the underside of British ships. The *Turtle* failed in its mission. But successful submarines were later based on the *Turtle's* design.

WEAPONS, GEAR, AND UNIFORMS

→ OF THE ←

CIVIL WAR

→THE U.S. CIVIL WAR←

In the early morning hours of April 12, 1861, heavy guns pounded Fort Sumter near Charleston, South Carolina. It was just the beginning of the bloodiest war in U.S. history. The U.S. Civil War (1861–1865) grew out of tensions concerning the end of slavery and keeping the country together. The Southern states' economy was based on farming and slavery. African-Americans had been held in slavery in the South for nearly 250 years.

The Northern states' economy was based on industrial manufacturing. Slaves weren't used in the factories. Many northerners felt slavery was wrong and should be stopped. But people in the South didn't want to free their slaves. They believed that states had the right to choose to be a slave state or a free state. Many heated debates took place in the U.S. Congress. People from the North and the South argued about slavery and states' rights for several years.

Beginning in 1860, several states chose to secede from the United States. They formed a new country called the Confederate States of America. However, President Abraham Lincoln wanted to keep the United States together as one nation. For the next four years, Union and Confederate soldiers fought a terrible war that cost more than half a million American lives.

FIVE MAJOR CIVIL WAR BATTLES

- **Battle of Shiloh, Tennessee**
  Fought: April 6–7, 1862
  Union casualties: 13,047
  Confederate casualties: 10,694

- **Battle of Antietam, Maryland**
  Fought: September 17, 1862
  Union casualties: 12,410
  Confederate casualties: 13,724

- **Battle of Chancellorsville, Virginia**
  Fought: April 27–May 6, 1863
  Union casualties: 16,845
  Confederate casualties: 12,764

- **Battle of Gettysburg, Pennsylvania**
  Fought: July 1–3, 1863
  Union casualties: 23,055
  Confederate casualties: 28,063

- **Battle of Chickamauga, Georgia**
  Fought: August 16–September 22, 1863
  Union casualties: 16,170
  Confederate casualties: 18,454

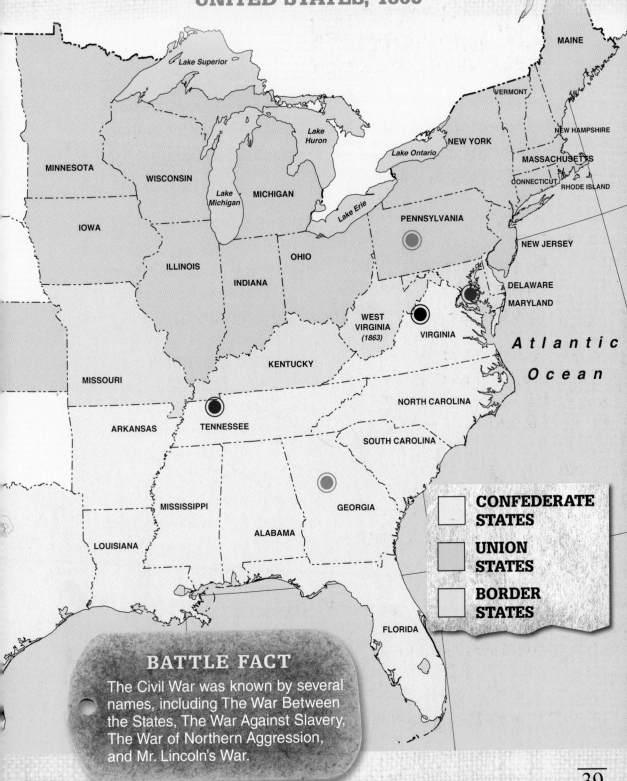

UNITED STATES, 1865

MAINE

Lake Superior

VERMONT

NEW HAMPSHIRE

MINNESOTA

WISCONSIN

Lake Huron

NEW YORK

MASSACHUSETTS

CONNECTICUT

RHODE ISLAND

MICHIGAN

Lake Michigan

Lake Ontario

IOWA

Lake Erie

PENNSYLVANIA

NEW JERSEY

OHIO

DELAWARE

ILLINOIS

INDIANA

MARYLAND

WEST VIRGINIA (1863)

VIRGINIA

Atlantic

Ocean

MISSOURI

KENTUCKY

NORTH CAROLINA

ARKANSAS

TENNESSEE

SOUTH CAROLINA

MISSISSIPPI

GEORGIA

LOUISIANA

ALABAMA

FLORIDA

CONFEDERATE STATES

UNION STATES

BORDER STATES

BATTLE FACT

The Civil War was known by several names, including The War Between the States, The War Against Slavery, The War of Northern Aggression, and Mr. Lincoln's War.

UNION UNIFORMS

A soldier's weapons, clothing, and gear were key to surviving the war. The Union army's dress code detailed the style, color, and type of clothes soldiers wore. Each branch of the military used slightly different versions of a standard uniform.

FORAGE CAPS

Most Union infantry soldiers wore a forage cap made from dark blue wool. They were based on a French military hat called a kepi.

INFANTRY UNIFORMS

Union officers and soldiers were given long wool dress coats. But many soldiers preferred wearing more comfortable sack coats. These short coats had a turnover collar and an inside left pocket. Soldiers also wore light blue pants, a dark wool shirt, socks, long underwear, and tough leather shoes.

UNIFORM BUTTONS

Buttons were often stamped with an eagle with spread wings. Officers' buttons were marked with I, C, or A, which stood for Infantry, Cavalry, or Artillery.

CAVALRY SOLDIER UNIFORMS

Union cavalry uniform pants were reinforced in the seat and inside legs to prevent wear and tear from the saddle. Overcoats were made with a slit up the back to make riding and dismounting easier.

SLEEVE RANK BRAIDS

A Union officer's rank was shown with knotted braids on the sleeves of his overcoat. The rank of general had five braids in a double knot. A captain had two braids in a single knot.

BERDAN'S SHARPSHOOTERS

In 1861 Hiram Berdan formed the Sharpshooters. They were a group of expert marksmen known for their accurate shooting. They were nicknamed the "Green Coats" because they wore dark green coats. They also wore green pants.

CONFEDERATE UNIFORMS

At the start of the war, most Confederate soldiers didn't have official uniforms. The South didn't have factories to mass-produce uniforms. Soldiers often wore locally made clothing instead. Confederate uniforms were many different colors at first. A yellow-brown color called "butternut" was common. Later in the war, Confederate jackets were almost always gray.

INFANTRY UNIFORMS

The Southern uniform code originally called for a long gray coat. However, a short, waist-length coat replaced it. Confederate troops were sometimes called "graybacks." Soldiers usually wore gray, yellow-brown, or blue pants. They also had white cotton shirts, socks, and leather shoes. Some wore a forage cap.

BATTLE FACT

Confederate soldiers often had trouble getting quality clothes. Many took uniforms off dead Union soldiers or from Union prisoners. They sometimes dyed Union uniforms to avoid being mistaken for a Union soldier.

CAVALRY SOLDIERS

Confederate cavalry units often did not follow an official dress code. Their clothes were usually plain gray or butternut in color.

BELT BUCKLES

Confederate belts often had oval-shaped belt plates. Confederate belts usually used the Confederate States' initials, C.S. However, some Confederate troops wore buckles that had their home state's initials on them.

ZOUAVE SOLDIERS

Both Union and Confederate armies had Zouave soldiers. These soldiers were specially trained with new combat methods that made them efficient in battle. Both Union and Confederate Zouaves wore bright-colored uniforms, baggy pants, and a forage cap.

Civil War soldiers carried much more than their weapons. They had to pack and carry all the gear they used daily. Soldiers carried their tents, blankets, canteens, and other necessities as they marched between battles.

HEAVY EQUIPMENT

Fully equipped soldiers had to carry 40 to 50 pounds (18 to 23 kg) of gear. Soldiers carried food, ponchos, mess kits, and personal items in a knapsack.

CONFEDERATE "BLANKETS"

Confederate soldiers often did not have blankets. Many used old carpet pieces as blankets instead.

CANTEENS

Union canteens were made from two dish-shaped parts that were welded together. They were covered in cloth and had a leather or canvas strap. Many Union canteens held close to 3 pints (1.4 l) of water. Confederate troops often carried canteens made from wood.

CARTRIDGE BOXES

Cartridge boxes were made from black leather. Inside were two tin compartments that held 40 black gunpowder cartridges. When filled, cartridge boxes weighed more than 3 pounds (1.4 kg). Soldiers carried the boxes on a waist belt.

IDENTITY DISCS

Union soldiers were not given official dog tags for identification. Instead, some soldiers bought identity discs that were made by jewelers. The discs were often advertised in newspapers or sold by civilian army suppliers called sutlers.

BATTLE FACT

Many soldiers could not afford identity discs. Instead, they simply wrote their names on a piece of paper. Soldiers would pin the papers onto their coats before going into battle.

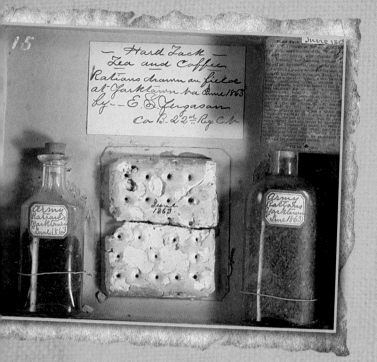

CIVIL WAR FOOD

Most soldiers ate a simple diet. They lived on bread, bacon, beans, dried potatoes, coffee, and sugar. They ate beef occasionally. However, the meat was often rotten and crawling with maggots. Soldiers also ate a tough crackerlike bread called hardtack.

GUM BLANKETS

A gum blanket was a piece of cloth coated with rubber. Soldiers usually used it as a rain cape. It could also be used as a floor for a small shelter called a pup tent. Soldiers sometimes drew game boards on them for playing games such as checkers.

MESS KITS

Soldiers were given mess kits by their home states. Each state had its own mess kit design. Mess kits usually included forks, spoons, knives, plates, and cups. A few included salt and pepper shakers.

McCLELLAN CAVALRY SADDLES

Union General George McClellan designed his own saddle before the war. The McClellan saddle was one of the most popular during the war. It was lightweight, sturdy, and inexpensive.

TENTS

Soldiers used various tents for shelter. A poncho tent was made with three rubber-coated blankets. It could hold three soldiers. Pup tents were not well-liked by most soldiers. They got their name because they were very small. Soldiers complained that only a small dog could stay dry in one.

RIFLES

At the start of the Civil War, many troops used basic muskets. They were inaccurate and often didn't hit their targets. But advances were made during the war. Rifles were faster to load than muskets. And they were more accurate. The new rifle designs helped soldiers shoot more enemies from a greater distance.

1861 SPRINGFIELD RIFLE

The Springfield was one of the most common rifles used in the war. The gun weighed about 9 pounds (4 kg) and was nearly 5 feet (1.5 m) long. A bayonet could be attached to the end, making the weapon more than 6 feet (1.8 m) long.

SHARPS RIFLE AND CARBINE

Sharps rifles and carbines were used mostly by Union soldiers. Troops could quickly load and fire these breech-loading guns. The rifle was 47 inches (119 cm) long and weighed 8.75 pounds (3.9 kg). The carbine was 39 inches (99 cm) long and weighed about 8 pounds (3.6 kg).

ENFIELD RIFLE MUSKET 1853

Both the Confederate and Union armies used Enfield rifles. The Enfield was made in England and imported to the United States. It weighed about 9 pounds (4 kg) and had a 33-inch (84-cm) barrel.

HENRY REPEATING RIFLE

The Henry was the most advanced rifle used by the Union in the war. It weighed about 9 pounds (4 kg) and had a 24-inch (61-cm) long barrel. Its magazine held 15 rounds, which could all be fired in less than 11 seconds. It was not an official weapon. Union soldiers usually had to buy the rifle with their own money.

SPENCER RIFLE

The Spencer rifle was a seven-shot repeater rifle. It was 47 inches (119 cm) long and weighed 10 pounds (4.5 kg). A well-trained marksman could fire all seven shots in 12 seconds.

BATTLE FACT

Christopher M. Spencer invented the Spencer rifle in 1860. President Lincoln tested the rifle himself near the White House. Lincoln was impressed with the rifle's accuracy. He soon ordered as many of these weapons as Spencer's factory could provide.

HANDGUNS

   Along with rifles, soldiers carried handguns. Small guns were useful when a soldier ran out of ammunition for his rifle. Both the Union and Confederate armies used a wide variety of handguns. Navy guns usually fired .36-caliber bullets, while army guns used .44-caliber bullets.

COLT MODEL 1851 NAVY REVOLVER

The Colt 1851 Navy revolver was made from 1850 to 1873. It was a .36-caliber revolver that held six shots. Its 7.5-inch (19-cm) barrel was shaped like an octagon.

COLT MODEL 1861 NAVY REVOLVER

The 1861 revolver was identical to the Model 1851, except that its barrel was round.

SHOULDER STOCKS

Colt made shoulder stock attachments for some of their handguns. A shoulder stock helped make a gun more stable as it was fired. The Model 1851 came with a shoulder stock that contained a canteen.

COLT MODEL 1860 ARMY REVOLVER

The 1860 Army revolver was a six-shot
.44-caliber handgun. The dependable weapon
was the main handgun used by Union troops.
It was about 14 inches (36 cm) long.

LeMAT "GRAPESHOT" REVOLVER

The LeMat revolver was used mainly by the Confederate
army. It had two barrels. The secondary smoothbore barrel
could fire a shotgun load of small pellets. The gun was
known as the "Grapeshot" revolver because of this feature.

AUGUSTA MACHINE WORKS REVOLVER

The Confederacy didn't have many real Colt revolvers. Instead, they
copied the pattern without Colt's approval. The end result was a
nearly identical gun called the Augusta Machine Works revolver.

BLADES AND GRENADES

Civil War soldiers also used swords, bayonets, and grenades in battle. However, both sides quickly learned that edged weapons were of little use against guns. Soldiers often used their blades for everyday tasks instead, such as opening cans or holding meat over an open fire. Sometimes bayonets were even used as stakes or pins for soldiers' tents.

LIGHT CAVALRY SABER MODEL 1860

This sword's blade was 34 inches (86 cm) long and was slightly curved. The weapon had a hand guard made of brass. The grip was covered in black leather that was tied with brass wire.

CONFEDERATE SWORD

Confederate swords were usually copies of Union swords. However, they were often made from low-quality materials.

CONFEDERATE BAYONETS

Like many Confederate weapons, Southern bayonets were copies of Union models. But the quality was not as good. Some bayonets had steel only in their tips. The rest of the blades were made from iron, which could break easily.

KETCHUM'S GRENADE

The Ketchum's grenade came in 1-, 3-, and 5-pound (0.5-, 1.4-, and 2.3-kg) sizes. It had a wooden tail with cardboard fins to help it land and explode correctly.

HAYNES "EXCELSIOR" HAND GRENADE

The Haynes grenade was a cast-iron ball with an inner and an outer shell. The inner shell held the explosive powder. The Haynes was made to explode on impact after being thrown. Its outer shell would explode into deadly fragments.

Armies pounded enemy troops with artillery weapons such as cannons, mortars, and howitzers during the war. These guns were large and heavy. It took a small group of soldiers to move, load, and fire these powerful weapons. The guns could fire large ammunition to destroy enemy targets from long distances.

12-POUNDER NAPOLEON MODEL 1857

Both the Union and Confederacy used the Napoleon cannon. It weighed 1,227 pounds (557 kg), not including the two-wheeled carriage it sat on. The Napoleon could fire twice per minute, and it could hit targets nearly 1 mile (1.6 km) away.

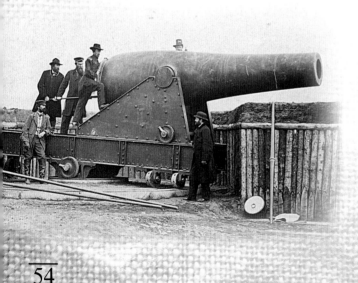

THOMAS J. RODMAN SMOOTHBORE COLUMBIAD

The Thomas J. Rodman Columbiad was one of the largest cannons ever made. It weighed 117,000 pounds (53,000 kg). The huge gun could fire a 1,080-pound (490-kg) shell at targets up to 4.5 miles (7.2 km) away.

10-POUNDER PARROTT

The Parrott cannon had a rifled cast-iron tube. An iron hoop strengthened the breech at the rear of the gun.

WHITWORTH 12-POUNDER

The Whitworth cannon was mainly used by the Confederacy. It fired an unusual six-sided shell called a "bolt." The gun's unique shells and design made it very accurate.

MORTARS

Mortars were made to sit low to the ground. They fired heavy balls high into the sky. The ammunition then landed and exploded behind enemy lines. Mortars were used at both the battles of Vicksburg and Petersburg.

STAKE TORPEDO

The stake torpedo was a land mine that held about 50 pounds (23 kg) of explosive powder. It was positioned at an angle and held in place with an anchor attached to its upper end.

GRAPESHOT/CANISTER SHOT

Two of the deadliest forms of cannon ammunition were canister and grapeshot. A tin canister was filled with 27 cast-iron balls, each weighing about 0.5 pound (0.23 kg). The canister was then fired from a smoothbore cannon. Grapeshot included nine large iron balls wrapped in cloth or canvas.

BATTLE FACT

Land torpedoes were like modern-day land mines. Known as "sensitive shells," they were usually buried in the ground and exploded when stepped on.

COAL TORPEDO

Coal torpedoes were actually small bombs. Hollow pieces of iron were filled with explosive powder. Then they were covered in tar and coal dust to look like coal. They were hidden in coal depots where Union ships got the coal to power their engines. When the torpedoes were thrown into a ship's furnace, they would explode and damage the ship.

SWAMP ANGEL CANNON

The Union used this big Parrott cannon to attack the city of Charleston, South Carolina, on August 22, 1863. The gun fired 200-pound (91-kg) shells from a floating platform on a marsh at the mouth of Charleston Harbor.

WHISTLING DICK

The Whistling Dick had a rifled barrel. It got its nickname from the sound its ammunition made. The 18-pound (8.2-kg) shell made a whistling sound as it flew through the air.

UNION AND CONFEDERATE NAVIES

In 1861 both the Union and Confederacy had only a few ships. But by the end of the war, the Union had 671 ships, while the Confederacy had about 500 vessels. Both sides also began making ironclad ships. These warships were covered with sheets of iron armor to protect against enemy fire.

CSS *VIRGINIA*

From 1861 to 1862, the South rebuilt the wrecked Union ship USS *Merrimack* into the ironclad battleship the CSS *Virginia*. It was about 263 feet (80 m) long. It had 10 heavy guns. It was the first ironclad ship made by the Confederacy.

BATTLE FACT

The *Monitor* and the *Virginia* clashed on March 9, 1862. It was the first battle between two ironclad warships. The battle was fought to a draw.

USS *MONITOR*

The USS *Monitor* was the first ironclad ship built by the Union. It was 179 feet (55 m) long. It sat low in the water, with only about 18 inches (46 cm) of the hull above the water's surface. It had a turret on top that contained two powerful 11-inch (28-cm) guns.

CSS *H.L. HUNLEY* SUBMARINE

The Confederate submarine CSS *H.L. Hunley* was made in part from an old boiler. It was about 40 feet (12 m) long and about 4 feet (1.2 m) wide. It was powered manually by eight men sitting at eight cranks on the end of a propeller shaft. The *H.L. Hunley* is known as the first submarine to sink an enemy ship during wartime.

UNION GUNBOATS

Union gunboats patrolled rivers. The boats were powered by side-wheels that allowed them to move through shallow river waters. Gunboats were heavily armed with cannons. Many were covered with armor 1.5 to 2 inches (3.8 to 5.1 cm) thick. A few gunboats had poor armor and were called "tinclads."

MACHINE GUNS, VOLLEY GUNS, AND ROCKETS

Machine guns and rockets were introduced during the Civil War but were not widely used. Early machine guns often became jammed and had other malfunctions. Rockets could be unpredictable.

BILLINGHURST-REQUA BATTERY GUN

The Billinghurst-Requa was made from 25 rifle barrels placed side by side on a wooden frame. It was carried on a lightweight carriage. It was called a covered bridge gun because it was often used to defend covered bridges.

AGER "COFFEE MILL" MACHINE GUN

The Ager machine gun was nicknamed the "Coffee Mill." It used a hand crank that looked similar to the kind used on coffee grinders at the time. The gun could fire 120 rounds per minute.

GATLING GUN

The Gatling gun had six barrels that rotated with a crank. It could fire more than 200 rounds per minute.

HALE ROCKET

The Hale rocket had three curved vanes at its base to make it spin while in flight. The spinning motion kept it stable as it flew. It could travel up to 1 mile (1.6 km).

WILLIAMS "ONE-POUNDER" MACHINE GUN

The Williams machine gun could fire 65 1-pound (0.5-kg) rounds per minute. It had a range of 2,000 yards (1,829 m). This gun was used in the Battle of Seven Pines in 1862.

VANDENBERG VOLLEY GUN

The Vandenberg volley gun was developed during the war, but saw little use. It had between 85 and 451 barrels. The number of barrels depended on the size of ammunition being used. The weapon was fired by a charge that set off all the barrels at the same time.

EQUIPPED FOR BATTLE

WEAPONS, GEAR, AND UNIFORMS

✦ OF ✦

WORLD WAR I

★ WORLD WAR I ★

The early 1900s saw a lot of tension among countries in Europe. Britain, France, and Germany all wanted to be the most powerful nation in the world. Austria-Hungary and Russia competed to control parts of eastern Europe. And the United States was also growing into a world power. The friction between countries eventually led to events that would erupt into war.

World War I (1914–1918) began with the assassination of Austria's Archduke Franz Ferdinand. Austria accused Serbia of a plot to murder him. Other nations quickly took sides. Germany supported Austria. Russia, France, and Great Britain came to the defense of Serbia. The United States did not join the war until 1917. But U.S. forces helped determine the war's outcome.

Most nations thought the war would be short. But it turned into one of the longest and costliest wars ever fought. Bloody battles raged across Europe, the Middle East, Africa, and Asia for four years.

Armies began using several new weapons during the war. Tanks were widely used in war for the first time. Soldiers on both sides feared deadly new gas weapons. More than 37 million soldiers were killed, wounded, or went missing during the war. The horrific fighting led the conflict to be called "The War to End All Wars."

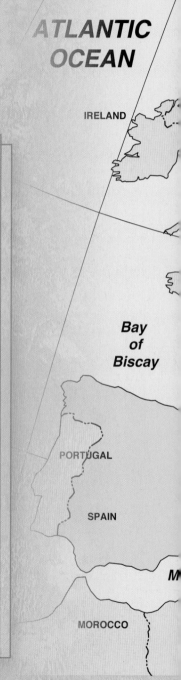

ATLANTIC OCEAN

IRELAND

Bay of Biscay

PORTUGAL

SPAIN

MOROCCO

FOUR MAJOR WORLD WAR I BATTLES

⬤ **FIRST BATTLE OF YPRES**
Fought: October 18, 1914–November 22, 1914
Allied Powers casualties: about 160,000
Central Powers casualties: about 130,000

◯ **GALLIPOLI CAMPAIGN**
Fought: April 25, 1915–January 9, 1916
Allied Powers casualties: more than 280,000
Central Powers casualties: about 250,000

◉ **BATTLE OF VERDUN**
Fought: February 21, 1916–December 18, 1916
Allied Powers casualties: about 370,000
Central Powers casualties: about 340,000

◉ **BATTLE OF THE SOMME**
Fought: July 1, 1916–November 18, 1916
Allied Powers casualties: more than 620,000
Central Powers casualties: about 500,000

ALLIED AND CENTRAL POWERS IN EUROPE, 1914

NORWAY

SWEDEN

Gulf of Finland

North Sea

DENMARK

Baltic Sea

UNITED KINGDOM

NETH.

BELGIUM

LUX.

GERMAN EMPIRE

RUSSIA

AUSTRIA-HUNGARY

SWITZERLAND

FRANCE

ITALY

Adriatic Sea

ROMANIA

Black Sea

SERBIA

BULGARIA

MONTENEGRO

ALBANIA

GREECE

OTTOMAN EMPIRE

Aegean Sea

Tyrrhenian Sea

Mediterranean Sea

ALGERIA

TUNISIA

N W E S

ALLIED POWERS

CENTRAL POWERS

NEUTRAL NATIONS

At the beginning of World War I, some armies dressed their soldiers in brightly colored uniforms. The colorful clothing made it easier for soldiers to see one another on the battlefield. But that soon changed after fighting broke out in Europe. Being hard to see on a battlefield became a matter of survival.

ALLIED POWERS UNIFORMS

FRENCH UNIFORMS

At the start of the war, French soldiers wore brightly colored uniforms. Their clothes included a dark blue overcoat, red pants, and flat-topped kepi hats. But by May 1915, they began wearing standard blue uniforms that were harder for the enemy to spot.

RUSSIAN UNIFORMS

Russian soldiers wore light olive-green uniforms and a peaked cap. They also wore heavy hats during winter. The hats had flaps that could be used to cover soldiers' ears and necks. Rough wool greatcoats could also be used as cloaks or blankets.

BRITISH UNIFORMS

British soldiers wore basic khaki uniforms. The uniforms included single-breasted tunics with folding collars. There were also pants, puttees, and ankle boots. The khaki peaked cap sometimes had ear and neck flaps.

U.S. UNIFORMS

U.S. soldiers also wore khaki uniforms. An overseas cap was issued to troops sent to other countries. But when soldiers faced battle, they wore steel helmets and gas masks instead.

BATTLE FACT

Some Scottish troops went into battle wearing kilts. These heavy, knee-length wool skirts were usually made with a plaid pattern woven into them.

CENTRAL POWERS UNIFORMS

GERMAN UNIFORMS

German soldiers wore gray-green uniforms that included a single-breasted tunic with eight buttons. The pants were worn with knee boots. At the start of the war, German soldiers wore spiked helmets made of leather. But by 1916 these helmets were replaced with steel helmets that did a better job of protecting soldiers from shrapnel.

GERMAN HELMETS WITH STEEL BROW PLATES

German soldiers with very dangerous jobs had a steel plate strapped to the front of their helmets. These brow plates gave soldiers added protection, but were very heavy. The helmet and plate combined weighed more than 13 pounds (5.9 kg).

OTTOMAN EMPIRE UNIFORMS

Turkish soldiers from the Ottoman Empire wore German-style uniforms that were a greenish-khaki color. They included a single-breasted tunic with a folding collar, breeches, and puttees.

AUSTRO-HUNGARIAN UNIFORMS

When the war began, the Austro-Hungarian army wore blue-gray uniforms. However, by 1916 the uniforms changed to be similar to those worn by the German military.

ROYAL HUNGARIAN ARMY UNIFORMS

These uniforms were very similar to regular Austro-Hungarian soldiers' clothes. However, the belt buckle had the Hungarian coat of arms. The long tight-fitting pants also had Hungarian knots on the thighs and braiding down the outside seam.

BULGARIAN UNIFORMS

Bulgarian soldiers wore gray-green uniforms that looked similar to Russian uniforms. However, because of shortages, they were not worn by all soldiers. Some wore German uniforms. Bulgarian soldiers sometimes wore caps with a black or gray-green leather peak and chin strap.

TRENCH WARFARE

Across much of Europe, soldiers on both sides lived and fought in deep trenches. Life in the trenches was a nightmare. Rats and filthy water constantly led to diseases. Poison gas was first used as part of trench warfare. To survive the deadly gas, armies on both sides carried gas masks for protection.

EARLY GAS MASKS

Early French and British gas masks were basically goggles and a gauze pad. Later, flannel hoods with eyepieces were used.

WIRE CUTTERS

Barbed wire often covered the area between opposing trenches, which was known as "no-man's-land." Soldiers used wire cutters to cut through the wire and cross over this area. There were several kinds of wire cutters. They included folding cutters and cutters that fit on the barrel of a rifle.

GERMAN GAS MASKS

German gas masks were made from rubber-coated cloth or oiled leather. They were hot and uncomfortable to wear. They also didn't protect soldiers well against large amounts of gas.

SMALL BOX RESPIRATORS

These British gas masks had shatterproof eyepieces. Special valves allowed soldiers to breath without making the eyepieces fog up. The masks protected soldiers from all gases except mustard gas.

BATTLE FACT

The Germans launched the first gas attack of the war on April 22, 1915, at Ypres, Belgium.

TRENCH PERISCOPES

Handheld periscopes were an important tool for soldiers fighting in trenches. Periscopes allowed soldiers to watch their enemies while staying protected in the trenches.

PORTABLE FIELD TELEPHONES

Portable field telephones were often carried in a leather shoulder bag. The phone came with keys used for sending Morse code. Morse code was used when soldiers were in battle and couldn't hear the speaker at the other end of the phone.

CARRIER PIGEONS

Sometimes trained pigeons were the only way soldiers on the front lines could communicate with headquarters. Soldiers tied messages to the pigeons' legs and then sent them back to commanding officers.

BATTLE FACT

France gave the Legion of Honor award to a carrier pigeon. The bird had carried out its mission after being exposed to poison gas. It died soon after it delivered the message.

DOG MESSENGERS

Dogs were often used to carry messages between trenches. The messages were kept in tubes on the dogs' collars. The dogs were trained to leap over barbed wire. The dogs ran fast and were hard for snipers to shoot.

STAR SHELLS

Star shells were magnesium flares that burned brightly when fired into the air. They were used as prearranged signals. The shells were different colors, and each had a specific meaning. The shells also provided light in no-man's-land so enemy movements could be seen at night.

MESS KITS

Soldiers usually carried mess kits for eating their meals. A kit included a cup, a spoon, and a fork. Some kits also had containers to hold alcohol and chocolate rations.

Rifles and handguns became much more accurate and reliable during the war. Many of the rifles used by warring nations were similar in their basic designs. The rifles used magazines and bolt-action loading systems. These systems could eject a used shell and load a new one at the same time. This design allowed soldiers to keep firing without manually reloading their rifles.

RIFLES

SPRINGFIELD RIFLES

U.S. soldiers mainly used 1903 Springfield rifles. These guns could fire bullets at 2,700 feet (823 m) per second. The gun came with a five-round clip, weighed 8.5 pounds (3.9 kg), and was 3.6 feet (1.1 m) long. It was one of the lightest and shortest rifles used in the war.

LEBEL 1893 MODEL RIFLES

The French army used the Lebel 1893 rifle. Its magazine held eight rounds. The Lebel was the heaviest of all the basic rifles used in the war. It weighed 9.2 pounds (4.2 kg) and measured 4.3 feet (1.3 m) long.

MODEL 1891 MOSIN-NAGANT RIFLES

The 1891 Mosin-Nagant weighed 9 pounds (4.1 kg) and was 4.3 feet (1.3 m) long. It was very popular with Russian troops. Russian factories produced 111,000 of these rifles a month, but it still wasn't enough to meet demand.

MODEL 1898 MAUSER RIFLES

German 1898 Mauser rifles were longer and heavier than British and U.S. rifles. They were 4.1 feet (1.2 m) long and weighed about 9 pounds (4.1 kg).

GERMAN ANTI-TANK GUNS

Nicknamed the "Elephant Gun," this anti-tank gun was used by Germany. The 20 mm rounds could pierce armor up to 1.2 inches (3 cm) thick. The gun weighed 109 pounds (49 kg).

LEE ENFIELD .303 RIFLES

Lee Enfield rifles were used mainly by British forces. They used 10-cartridge magazines. The rifle weighed 8.7 pounds (3.9 kg).

HANDGUNS AND EDGED WEAPONS

WEBLEY MARK VI
.455-CALIBER REVOLVERS

The British-made Webley .455-caliber
revolver fired six rounds. It had a
6-inch (15.2-cm) barrel.

STEYR 9-MM AUTOMATIC PISTOLS

The Steyr pistol was the official handgun of
the Austro-Hungarian and Romanian armies.
Its magazine held eight rounds.

GERMAN LUGERS

German Lugers were often considered one
of the best handguns of the war. These
automatic pistols fired 9-mm bullets. The
Luger weighed 2 pounds (0.9 kg) and
had a 4-inch (10.2-cm) barrel. The gun's
magazine held eight rounds.

M1911 PISTOLS

The Browning-Colt Model 1911 was used mainly by U.S. forces. The pistol weighed 2 pounds (0.9 kg) and had a 5-inch (12.7-cm) barrel. Its magazine held seven rounds.

GERMAN BAYONETS

The German double-edged bayonet was 10.25 inches (26 cm) long. It weighed 0.5 pound (0.23 kg) and was made to fit onto the Mauser Gewehr 1898 rifle. Many German soldiers used these bayonets while fighting in hand-to-hand combat. The blades were not official German army weapons, but soldiers were still allowed to use them.

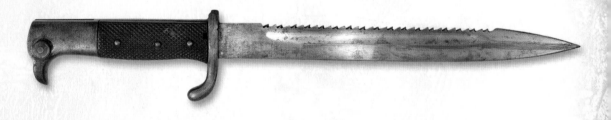

RUSSIAN MODEL 1907 TROOPER DAGGERS

Russian trooper daggers had carved handles. The blades were more than 17 inches (43 cm) long. Some Russian troops fought with these daggers instead of bayonets.

GRENADES, TRENCH CLUBS, AND FLAMETHROWERS

Grenades, flamethrowers, and clubs were important in trench warfare. Grenades came in many shapes and sizes. They could look like lightbulbs, lemons, apples, or even discs. Allied soldiers used grenades that looked like small pineapples. By the end of the war, Britain had produced at least 75,000,000 grenades.

GERMAN STICK GRENADE

Because of their appearance, German stick grenades were often called "potato mashers." This weapon had a fuse loaded into its hollow handle that could be lit by pulling a cord.

BATTLE FACT

About 1.5 billion shells were fired on the Western Front. French farmers are still finding unexploded grenades and shells in the ground today.

BRITISH MILLS GRENADES

The British used different models of the Mills grenade. These early grenades were very dangerous. The Mills Mark II often exploded in the hand of the thrower. In 1916 accidents were reduced when soldiers began using the Mark III.

TRENCH CLUBS

Hand-to-hand combat in the trenches was brutal. Trench clubs were often handmade weapons. Soldiers made them from various materials like nails, spikes, and metal rods. The clubs were used during night raids on enemy trenches.

FLAMETHROWERS

Flamethrowers used a mix of oil and gasoline that was shot out under pressure. The flamethrower could blast fire for two minutes at a distance of 60 feet (18.3 m). Flamethrowers were first used in combat on February 26, 1915. The Germans used them against French forces near Verdun, France.

★ HEAVY WEAPONS ★

World War I saw the first regular use of many heavy weapons and combat vehicles. These heavy weapons were capable of causing mass destruction on a scale never seen before.

MACHINE GUNS AND HEAVY FIELD GUNS

75 MM FIELD GUNS

These heavy field guns weighed 2,657 pounds (1,205 kg). They could fire 16-pound (7.3-kg) shells more than 4 miles (6.4 km). The gun normally fired six rounds per minute. But when needed, it could fire up to 20 rounds per minute. The gun was used at the Battle of the Marne to stop German advances in France.

HOTCHKISS MACHINE GUNS

Hotchkiss guns were the only air-cooled, gas-operated heavy machine guns in the war. They weighed 52 pounds (24 kg) and were often  used as anti-aircraft weapons. The United States used the Hotchkiss more than its own Browning machine gun.

BRITISH MARK I 60-POUNDER FIELD GUNS

The Mark I was Britain's largest field gun. A team of horses was required to pull it into position. It fired 60-pound (27-kg) shells at targets nearly 6 miles (9.7 km) away. The British used the Mark I at the Battle of the Somme.

BIG BERTHA

Big Bertha was a 420 mm howitzer. The German gun weighed 75 tons (68 metric tons) and had a crew of 280 soldiers. The giant gun could fire shells weighing 2,052 pounds (931 kg) at targets up to 9 miles (14.5 km) away.

GERMAN MAXIM MG 08 MACHINE GUNS

German Maxim MG 08 machine guns weighed 36 pounds (16.3 kg) and had a 2.6-foot (0.8-m) long barrels. These guns could fire up to 500 rounds per minute. The barrel was covered with a cooling jacket that held 5 pints (2.4 l) of water to help keep the barrel cool.

TANKS

When Britain began using tanks in battle, it changed the course of the war. The first tank assault happened on September 15, 1916, between the Somme and Ancre Rivers in France. The Allies' tanks surprised about 300 German troops in their trenches and forced them to surrender.

BRITISH MARK I

Mark I tanks came in two versions. The "male" was armed with two 6-pound (2.7-kg) guns and four machine guns. The "female" had seven machine guns. They each carried a crew of eight.

BRITISH MARK IV

The Mark IV tank could reach speeds of 3.5 miles (5.6 km) per hour. It had 57 mm guns, and 0.5-inch (1.3-cm) thick armor. Mark IV tanks were used at Cambrai, France, on November 20, 1917.

THE WHIPPET

The British Whippet tank had a gun turret at the rear, and it carried four Hotchkiss machine guns. Its two engines each powered one of the tank's tracks. The Whippet was small enough to be operated by a single soldier in an emergency.

GERMAN A7V TANKS

Germany's A7V tank was the only German-made tank in the war. It was armed with six heavy machine guns and a 57 mm cannon. The A7V took part in the first tank-against-tank battle of the war on April 24, 1918.

FRENCH SCHNEIDER TANKS

The Schneider was armed with one 75 mm gun and two Hotchkiss machine guns. These French tanks were first used in battle on April 16, 1917, at the beginning of the Nivelle Offensive in France.

RENAULT FT-17 TANKS

The French Renault FT-17 was the first tank with a turret that could turn around in a full circle. This design allowed the tank's two-man crew to fire in any direction.

85

SHIPS

Battleships existed long before World War I broke out. But warships greatly improved in size and firepower during the course of the war. The war also saw the birth of the naval aircraft carrier.

HMS *DREADNOUGHT*

The British warship HMS *Dreadnought* was armed with 12-inch (30.5-cm) guns mounted on twin turrets. It also carried 24 12-pound guns. The ship's success led the British navy to create the Dreadnought class warships.

SMS *NASSAU*

Germany built its own Dreadnought class battleships. The SMS *Nassau* was one of the first. It had twelve 11-inch (28-cm), twelve 5.9-inch (15-cm), and sixteen 3.4-inch (8.6-cm) guns. The *Nassau* entered the war in 1914. On May 31, 1916, the *Nassau* crashed into the British destroyer *Spitfire*, causing great damage and nearly destroying the British ship.

HMS *QUEEN ELIZABETH*

The HMS *Queen Elizabeth* was a super-dreadnaught class ship that carried a crew of 1,016. It carried eight 15-inch (38-cm) guns, twelve 6-inch (15-cm) guns, and twelve 12-pounders. The ship's armor was 13 inches (33 cm) thick. The *Queen Elizabeth* fought in the Mediterranean and North Seas.

BRITISH M-1 SUBMARINES

British M class submarines were 300 feet (91 m) long. They were armed with four 18-inch (46-cm) torpedo tubes. M-1 subs also carried a 12-inch (31-cm) gun. The sub fired an 850-pound (386-kg) shell that had to be loaded while on the water's surface.

GERMAN U-19 CLASS SUBMARINES

This diesel-powered submarine could travel about 4,000 miles (6,437 km) before refueling. A U-19 sub was responsible for sinking the British passenger ship RMS *Lusitania*. The U-19 carried four torpedo tubes and one 2-inch (5-cm) gun. It had a crew of 28 men.

AIRPLANES

Along with tanks and heavy guns, World War I also saw the first widespread use of airplanes in battle. The first military airplanes carried few weapons and only flew 50 to 75 miles (80 to 121 km) per hour. But by 1917, military airplanes were heavily armed with machine guns. They could also reach speeds of about 150 miles (240 km) per hour.

FOKKER DR-1

This German triplane was a favorite of German pilot Baron Manfred von Richthofen. The Fokker DR-1 could fly nearly 4 miles (6 km) high and up to 115 miles (185 km) per hour. Also known as the "Red Baron," Richthofen earned his nickname from his bright red plane. He painted it red so enemy pilots would know who shot them down.

BRITISH SOPWITH CAMELS

British Sopwith Camels had twin Vickers machine guns and could reach 122 miles (196 km) per hour. Some historians believe a Camel was responsible for shooting down Germany's famous "Red Baron" pilot on April 21, 1918.

BRISTOL F2B

The British-built Bristol F2B was armed with one fixed Vickers machine gun. It also carried one or two free-moving Lewis guns and twelve 20-pound (9-kg) bombs.

ALBATROS DIII

The German-built Albatross DIII was armed with two Spandau machine guns. The Albatross could reach speeds of 103 miles (166 km) per hour and could fly as high as 3.4 miles (5.5 km).

SPAD S XIII

The Spad S XIII was a French biplane fighter armed with two Vickers guns. It could fly up to 4 miles (6.6 km) high and as fast as 138 miles (222 km) per hour. Ace American pilot Eddie Rickenbacker flew a Spad for part of the war.

EQUIPPED FOR BATTLE

WEAPONS, GEAR, AND UNIFORMS

✠ OF ✠

WORLD WAR II

WORLD WAR II

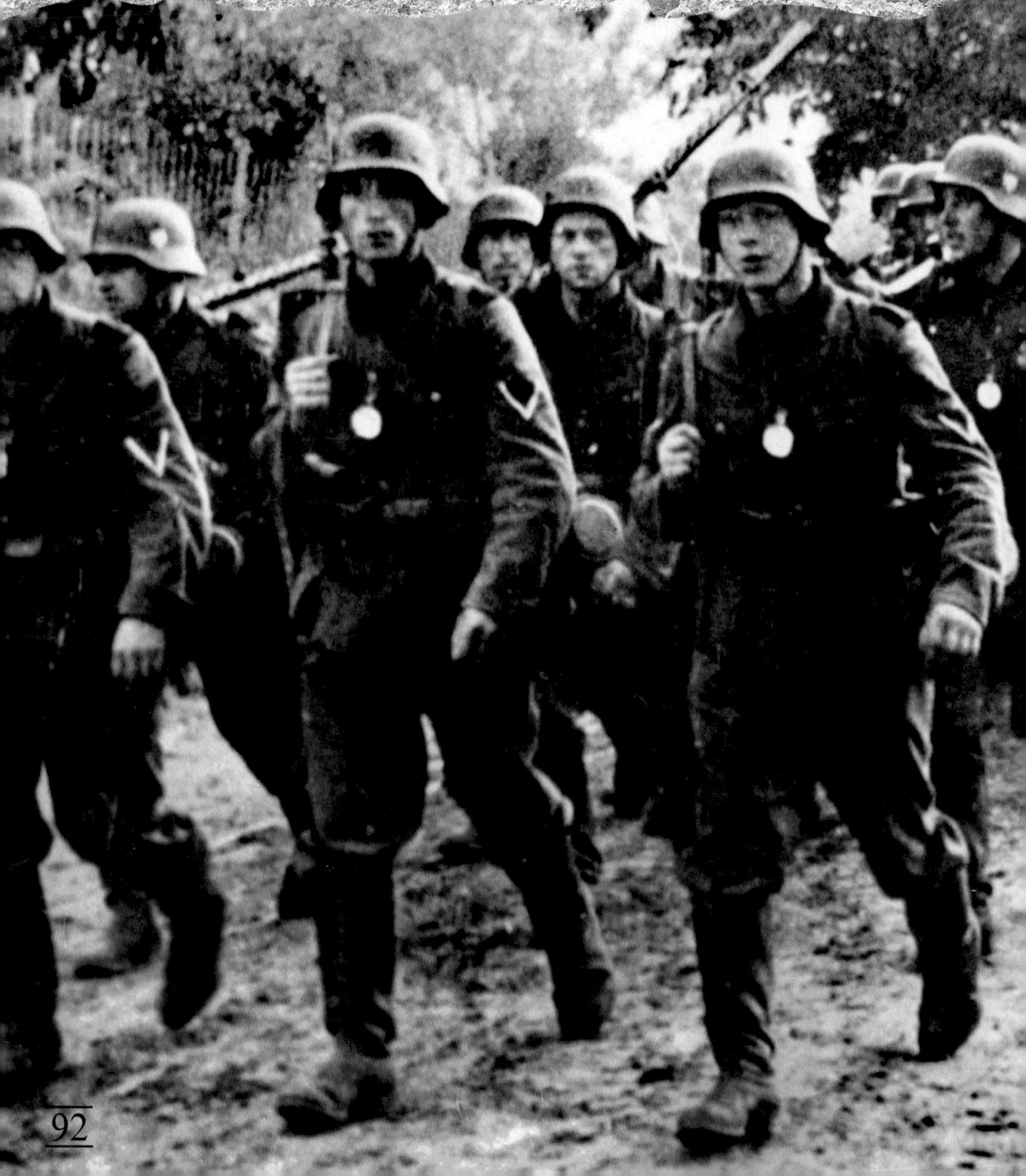

On September 1, 1939, German forces invaded Poland. It was the first military action of World War II (1939–1945). Taking over Poland was the first part of German leader Adolf Hitler's plan to control Europe. Italy later joined Germany to fight in Europe. Japan allied itself with Germany and fought in Asia and the Pacific. Together, these three major nations, and a few smaller countries, were known as the Axis powers.

Opposing them was a coalition of dozens of countries known as the Allies. The major Allied nations included Great Britain, France, the Soviet Union, and China. The United States joined the Allies in 1941. The Allies fought to defend themselves and to stop the Axis powers from taking over other nations.

World War II was the deadliest conflict the world has ever seen. Major battles raged across five continents and several oceans. By the time the war ended in 1945, more than 70 million people were dead. Millions more were homeless and starving. Never before had the world seen death and destruction on such a huge scale.

Several new weapons were developed during World War II. Many of them had the most advanced features of the time. Improved versions of tanks, rockets, and machine guns began to appear on the battlefield. But soldiers still used reliable older weapons and gear to survive in combat.

WORLD WAR II DEATHS
MILITARY AND CIVILIAN DEATHS*

NATION	TOTAL MILITARY CASUALTIES
China	14,500,000
France	563,000
Germany	6,500,000
Great Britain	357,000
Italy	395,000
Japan	1,900,000
Soviet Union	20,000,000
United States	298,000

* Accurate records of total deaths do not exist for several countries. Numbers listed are based on best estimates.

BATTLE FACT

On December 7, 1941, Japan launched a surprise attack on the U.S. naval base at Pearl Harbor, Hawaii. The attack brought the United States into World War II. More than 2,300 U.S. soldiers and sailors died at Pearl Harbor that day.

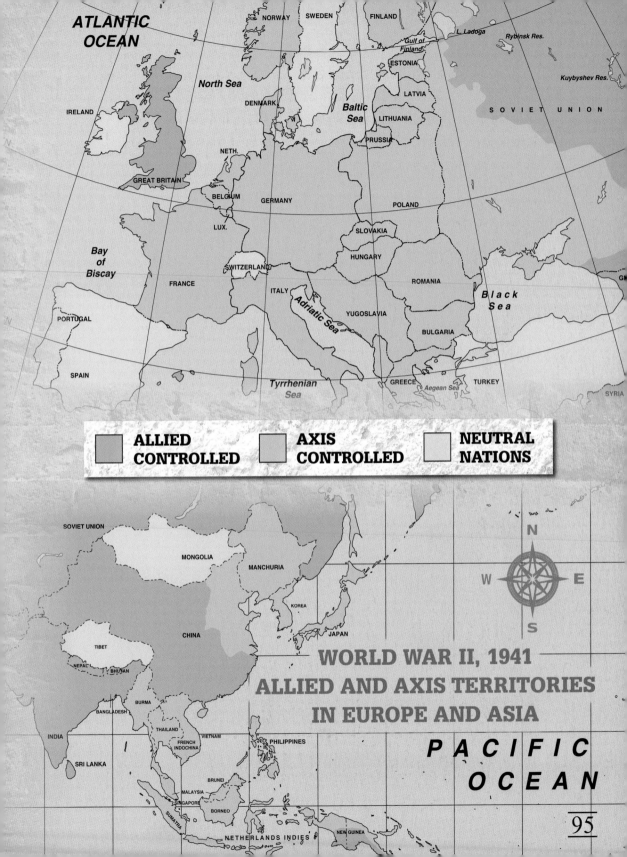

ATLANTIC OCEAN

NORWAY SWEDEN FINLAND
L. Ladoga
Rybinsk Res.
Gulf of Finland
ESTONIA
Kuybyshev Res.
North Sea
DENMARK
LATVIA
Baltic Sea
LITHUANIA
SOVIET UNION
IRELAND
PRUSSIA
NETH.
GREAT BRITAIN
BELGIUM
GERMANY
POLAND
LUX.
SLOVAKIA
Bay of Biscay
SWITZERLAND
HUNGARY
FRANCE
ITALY
ROMANIA
Black Sea
Adriatic Sea
YUGOSLAVIA
PORTUGAL
BULGARIA
SPAIN
Tyrrhenian Sea
GREECE
Aegean Sea
TURKEY
SYRIA

■ ALLIED CONTROLLED   ■ AXIS CONTROLLED   □ NEUTRAL NATIONS

SOVIET UNION
MONGOLIA
MANCHURIA
CHINA
KOREA
JAPAN
TIBET
NEPAL
BHUTAN
BURMA
BANGLADESH
THAILAND
VIETNAM
PHILIPPINES
INDIA
FRENCH INDOCHINA
SRI LANKA
BRUNEI
MALAYSIA
SINGAPORE
BORNEO
SUMATRA
NEW GUINEA
NETHERLANDS INDIES

WORLD WAR II, 1941
ALLIED AND AXIS TERRITORIES
IN EUROPE AND ASIA

PACIFIC OCEAN

N W E S

95

✠ UNIFORMS AND GEAR ✠

    Uniforms on both sides varied depending on a soldier's specific rank and job. Clothes made with certain color patterns called camouflage were common. Camouflage made it harder for enemies to see soldiers. Men doing construction work or maintaining machinery commonly wore casual clothing. They often got dirty and needed simple, cheap uniforms.

U.S. HELMETS

For a U.S. infantry soldier, the most important part of the uniform was a metal helmet. Helmets came in different shapes, but all offered protection from enemy fire.

U.S. INFANTRY UNIFORMS

The typical U.S. soldier wore olive-colored pants and shirts. Canvas leggings covered the bottom part of the pants. As the war went on, most soldiers switched to high boots made of leather.

GERMAN INFANTRY UNIFORMS

German infantry troops typically wore gray-green uniforms. Uniform shirts, called field tunics, had four front pockets. When not in battle, the soldiers wore basic field caps.

OFFICERS' INSIGNIA

Officers from both sides wore insignia to show their rank. German naval captains had four gold bars and a gold star on their shirt cuffs. U.S. officers wore a variety of stripes and bars on their sleeves. High ranking U.S. officers like colonels and generals wore silver bars, eagles, or stars on their collars.

WOMEN'S DRESS UNIFORMS

During the war, several million women joined their country's military or found ways to help in the war effort. Women's formal uniforms usually included dresses or skirts.

SPECIALIZED UNIFORMS

Many troops faced extreme weather conditions. They fought in steamy jungles, freezing mountains, and hot deserts. Different climates forced both the Axis and Allied militaries to create specialized uniforms. Soldiers had to be protected from the weather and still be able to fight on the battlefield.

COOL CLOTHING

African deserts and Asian jungles could be very hot. Soldiers in these locations often wore shorts to beat the heat. Desert clothes were usually a light brown color to match the desert sands. Some soldiers also wore sun helmets with a wide brim that offered extra protection from the sun.

WADING SUITS

Some Soviet soldiers wore a special wading uniform. The suit helped soldiers cross rivers. It had rubber overalls that covered most of the body. The soldiers also wore an inflatable rubber tube around their waist.

LEATHER PILOT SUITS

Airplanes were unheated, so warm clothing was important for pilots. Pilots often wore leather clothing lined with a type of wool called fleece. Some pilots wore specialized suits that were heated by electricity.

FROGMEN

U.S. Navy divers called frogmen often wore simple swimsuits on their missions. The divers were nicknamed "naked warriors." Frogmen also wore large rubber flippers and plastic masks to help them move easily underwater.

WINTER COATS

Soldiers in cold winter climates often wore thick coats with hoods. The coats helped the men stay warm, but they often could not move easily on the battlefield. Winter clothing was sometimes white to blend in with the snow.

SPECIALIZED EQUIPMENT

Military forces in World War II needed many kinds of specialized gear to do their jobs. Officers used radios to communicate with soldiers on the battlefield. Troops injured in battle needed first-aid care. And some specialized equipment helped troops avoid deadly situations in the first place.

MINE DETECTORS

Both Axis and Allied forces buried land mines to blow up passing vehicles and troops. Some soldiers used mine detectors to locate these deadly devices. The first electronic mine detector was invented during the war. It used magnets and made a noise when it detected metal underground.

MEDICAL KITS

Medics were trained to treat serious battlefield injuries. Their kits contained bandages, medicine, medical knives, and tools to remove bullets. Most soldiers also carried smaller first-aid kits.

LIFE JACKETS

Life jackets were an important piece of safety equipment for sailors and pilots. The jackets kept the men floating if they ended up in the water. Some jackets were made with lightweight materials that floated easily. Other jackets filled with air when a cord was pulled.

BATTLE FACT

Spies on both sides used a variety of special tools. Spies could hide knives inside their shoes. Tiny cameras could be hidden inside matchboxes. Small, thin knives could fit inside pencils. These tools helped spies carry out dangerous missions deep in enemy territory.

FIELD RADIOS

Radio operators carried portable, battery-powered radios. One common U.S. model fit into a backpack. Radios greatly increased a commander's ability to direct his troops on the battlefield. Some radios sent their signals over wires. Soldiers carried rolls of radio wire onto the battlefield to connect commanders with their troops.

AXIS POWERS LIGHT GUNS AND BLADES

Axis soldiers used several different rifles, pistols, and bladed weapons. Soldiers sometimes fought with knives in hand-to-hand combat. Officers wore swords, but they were used mainly for ceremonies. Machine guns could fire hundreds of rounds of ammunition in only a few seconds.

MAUSER RIFLES

The German army commonly used Mauser rifles. Mauser clips typically held five bullets. After firing, the shooter slid a metal bar called a bolt to push a new bullet into the gun's chamber.

LUGER PISTOLS

German officers often carried Lugers. These semiautomatic pistols held eight bullets. The bullets were automatically loaded after each shot was fired. The Luger was well known as an accurate gun.

STURMGEWEHR MP44 SUBMACHINE GUNS

A submachine gun uses gases created inside the gun. The gases move a spring that ejects used casings and loads fresh bullets. Machine guns could be easily carried and fired by one person. The German MP44 had a magazine that held 30 bullets. It fired at a rate of 500 rounds per minute.

ARISAKA TYPE 38 CARBINES

Some soldiers used shorter bolt-action carbines. A soldier had to move the gun's bolt to load a bullet manually. The shorter barrel made it easier to carry. Japanese paratroopers often used the Arisaka Type 38 carbine.

TACHI SWORDS

Japanese officers carried a variety of swords, including the tachi. These swords were usually worn to honor the skills of ancient samurai warriors. But some officers were trained to use them in combat.

ALLIED POWERS LIGHT GUNS AND BLADES

Like the Axis powers, the Allies fought with a variety of handheld weapons such as bolt-action rifles and submachine guns. Some special forces carried out missions behind enemy lines. To avoid raising an alarm, they carried special knives that could take out enemies quickly and quietly.

COLT .45 PISTOLS

Most U.S. troops carried the Colt .45 semiautomatic pistol as a sidearm. It fired slightly larger bullets than the revolvers it replaced. This gun is still made today.

MOSIN-NAGANT M1891 SNIPER RIFLES

Snipers used powerful rifles such as the Soviet-made Mosin-Nagant. These guns allowed snipers to hide in a protected location and fire accurately on enemies from a distance. The Soviets made more than 300,000 of these rifles. Some came with telescopes that helped snipers shoot even more accurately.

BATTLE FACT

With a telescope, Mosin-Nagant rifles were accurate up to about 2,400 feet (732 m).

BROWNING AUTOMATIC RIFLES (BARS)

The Allies had machine guns of all sizes. One light machine gun was the Browning automatic rifle. It could fire at a rate of 500 rounds per minute. The rapid fire of a machine gun makes the barrel very hot. Some World War II machine guns used a water system to keep the barrel cool. But the Browning relied on air to stay cool.

STEN SUBMACHINE GUNS

British troops often used Sten submachine guns. The guns cost only about $10 to make. They were easy to use, but many soldiers didn't like them because they tended to be unreliable in combat.

COMBAT KNIVES

Both British and U.S. forces used "knuckleduster" knives. The handle had metal rings that fit around the fingers. If the soldier couldn't use the blade, he could still punch enemies with the metal rings. Another common combat knife was the Fairbairn-Sykes knife. This British knife had a deadly double-edged blade.

EXPLOSIVES AND SPECIALIZED WEAPONS

Millions of explosive devices were used during the war. Soldiers often carried hand grenades into battle. Land mines and sea mines were easily hidden to take out enemy troops and ships. Certain specialized weapons appeared for the first time during the war.

U.S. "PINEAPPLE" GRENADES

U.S. soldiers often used "pineapple" grenades, which got their nickname from the fruit they resemble. The thrower first pulled out a pin that kept a lever in place. Releasing the lever set off a four-second fuse. The grenade blew up four seconds after a soldier threw it.

GERMAN STICK GRENADES

German stick grenades were primed to explode by pulling a cord inside the wooden handle. The thrower had about four seconds to safely throw it at the enemy.

LAND MINES

These small explosives were buried underground. Some were designed to explode when enemy troops stepped on them. Larger land mines could take out tanks and other heavy vehicles.

FLAMETHROWERS

Flamethrowers were useful in driving enemy forces out of well-protected hiding places. The typical flamethrower used two tanks. One held fuel that was lit by a small flame at the end of the barrel. The other tank held a gas that forced the fuel out of the barrel. Both Axis and Allied forces used flamethrowers in the war.

BAZOOKAS

The U.S. military developed bazookas during the war. These weapons were light enough for one soldier to fire. The shells they launched were powerful enough to destroy a tank.

BATTLE FACT

About 300 million anti-tank mines were used during World War II. Countries are still discovering old, unexploded mines more than 70 years after the war ended.

MISSILES AND SMART BOMBS

In addition to small, handheld weapons, both sides used powerful artillery weapons. Field artillery sat on wheeled carriages and were towed by jeeps or trucks. Larger units were armored and could be driven like tanks. Howitzers and mortars were designed to fire over long distances or over tall objects.

SMALL ARTILLERY

Several countries developed small artillery. The German LG40 could be separated into several pieces and dropped by parachute from planes. Soldiers could use the powerful gun to launch surprise attacks behind enemy lines.

HOWITZERS

Howitzers were common in the war. These artillery units needed several men to load, aim, and fire their heavy shells. One large U.S. howitzer, nicknamed "Long Tom," could hit targets up to 13 miles (21 km) away.

KARL-GERÄT HOWITZERS

Germany created the largest of the self-propelled howitzers. The *Karl-Gerät* could fire a projectile that weighed nearly 5,000 pounds (2,268 kg).

NAVAL ARTILLERY

Battleships carried the largest naval guns. The guns sat in movable housings called turrets. Turrets could easily turn to fire at moving targets. They also protected the gun crew inside.

M1 MORTARS

The U.S.-made M1 mortar required a team of three to carry it and set it up. The M1 was sometimes used to fire smoke bombs that made it hard for enemy troops to see the battlefield.

SPECIALIZED HEAVY GUNS

Some heavy artillery pieces were designed for special tasks. Anti-aircraft (AA) guns were designed to accurately fire shells at enemy planes up to 7 miles (11 km) high. Anti-tank guns fired shells strong enough to pierce a tank's armor. Other heavy guns included cannons that sat on railroad cars and fired giant shells at targets miles away.

BRITISH MK III ANTI-AIRCRAFT GUNS

Powerful British 3.7-inch (9.4-cm) MK III guns fired 28-pound (13-kg) shells. They could hit targets up to 6 miles (9.7 km) high. Sometimes gunners used radar to help aim the gun.

GERMAN RAILWAY GUNS

During World War I (1914–1918), several armies used large artillery that had to be moved on railroad cars. Some of these were also used in World War II. Germany built most of these large guns. The K5 "Leopold" could fire a shell almost 39 miles (63 km).

BATTLE FACT

The largest railway gun of the war was nicknamed "Gustav." It could fire a 7-ton (6.4-metric ton) projectile up to 24 miles (39 km) away. It took hundreds of men and three weeks to assemble the German gun.

FLAK 88 ANTI-TANK GUN

With its wheels off, this German gun sat low to the ground. The Flak 88 was a semiautomatic gun. Its shells could pierce armor more than 6 inches (15 cm) thick.

BOFORS GUNS

Bofors anti-aircraft guns were used on land and at sea. The Swedish-built weapons could fire rapidly. However, their shells could only reach targets flying less than 1.4 miles (2.2 km) high.

TANKS

Tanks played a major role in battles across Europe. By using tracks instead of wheels, they could move easily off roads. Some armies took the basic tank frame and used it as the base for powerful tank destroyers. Some nations also relied on half-tracks, which had both tracks and wheels.

SHERMAN M4 TANKS

Sherman tanks weren't the most powerful, but U.S. factories built huge numbers of them. About 40,000 Shermans were built during the war. In addition to the main gun, Shermans carried several machine guns.

M3 HALF-TRACKS

Half-tracks were used to carry troops, anti-aircraft guns, and artillery. The vehicles were used by many Allied nations. They could move easily over wet ground and snow.

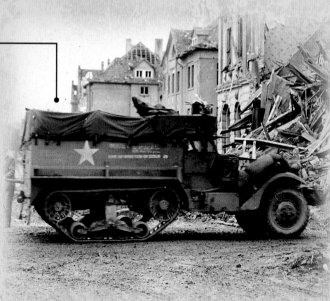

SOVIET T-34S

Military experts consider the T-34 one of the best tanks ever made. The Soviet-built tank combined speed, thick armor, and great firepower. These tanks were also easy to build, so they could be quickly replaced if destroyed in battle.

FUNNIES

The British made several specialized tanks. They were often called "funnies" because of their various designs. They included flame-throwing tanks, mine-sweeping tanks, and bulldozer-style tanks.

PANZER TIGERS

The German Panzer Tiger had an 88 mm gun. It was one of the largest guns on any tank of the war. The Tiger's thick armor helped protect it from enemy shells.

PLANES AND SHIPS

Airplanes were among the most important weapons used in the war. Bombers and fighters carried out countless missions. Meanwhile, ships also played a key role in many nations' war efforts. They carried troops, fired at land targets, launched aircraft, and battled other ships.

B-24 LIBERATORS

The B-24 Liberator flew missions everywhere the Allies fought. The U.S. bomber carried a crew of 10 and could fly a round trip of 3,000 miles (4,828 km). The plane also carried 10 machine guns to defend itself from enemy planes.

JAPANESE ZERO FIGHTER PLANES

Japanese Zero planes were some of the best fighters over the Pacific Ocean. The planes had a top speed of 310 miles (499 km) per hour. They were much faster than the U.S. fighters they faced.

LANDING CRAFT, MECHANIZED (LCM)

Landing craft, like the American-made LCM, were designed for amphibious attacks. They carried troops and equipment from large ships to shore.

AIRCRAFT CARRIERS

Aircraft carriers became the most important ships in naval fleets. With about 100 planes, carriers were like floating airfields. Each ship had a control center called an island on the top deck. Crews controlled takeoffs and landings of planes from the ship's island.

GERMAN U-BOATS

German submarines were known as U-boats, which stood for "undersea boats." U-boats carried a crew of 24 men. They were used to target the Allies' supply ships in the North Atlantic.

WARTIME INVENTIONS

Throughout history, new weapons have often made the difference between victory and defeat in war. During World War II, several nations introduced faster planes, large rockets, and radio-controlled bombs. And at the end of the war, the United States used the deadliest weapon ever invented—the atomic bomb.

V1 FLYING BOMBS

Germany's V1 flying bombs were powered by jet engines. They could fly about 400 miles (644 km) per hour. The V1 was nicknamed the "Buzz Bomb" because of the noise it made as it flew. It was used mostly to attack Great Britain, although some were also targeted at France and the Netherlands.

V2 ROCKET

Germany also built the first long-distance rocket. It could fly about 3,600 miles (5,794 km) per hour. It could deliver a 2,000-pound (907-kg) warhead. Some scientists who designed the V2 later worked on the U.S. program that sent rockets into space.

MESSERSCHMITT ME 262

In 1944 Germany began using the world's first fighter plane powered by a jet engine. The Messerschmitt ME 262 had a top speed of 540 miles (869 km) per hour. It flew about 100 miles (161 km) per hour faster than the best U.S. propeller planes. However, the ME 262 entered the war too late to have a major impact against the Allies.

THE ATOMIC BOMB

In 1945 the United States successfully created the first atomic bomb. In August of that year, the U.S. military dropped two atomic bombs on the Japanese cities of Hiroshima and Nagasaki. Japan surrendered soon afterward, bringing an end to World War II.

AFTER THE ATOMIC BOMB

A single atomic bomb equaled the explosive power of thousands of regular bombs. It also created a deadly form of energy called radiation. The atomic blasts in Japan, along with the resulting radiation, killed more than 300,000 people. The United States threatened to drop more atomic bombs on Japan. Facing total destruction, the Japanese government surrendered a few days after the second bomb blast.

EQUIPPED FOR BATTLE

WEAPONS, GEAR, AND UNIFORMS

✳ OF THE ✳

VIETNAM WAR

THE VIETNAM WAR

In 1954 Vietnam was split into North and South Vietnam. By 1955 war was brewing between the two countries. North Vietnam wanted communism. People there wanted North and South Vietnam to be a single communist country. The northern army was supported by the Soviet Union and China, two powerful communist countries.

People in South Vietnam wanted to keep their non-communist government. But South Vietnam's military forces were weak. The South didn't have enough troops and equipment to fight the North. People in South Vietnam asked the United States and other countries for help. U.S. leaders decided to help keep communism out of South Vietnam. At first the United States just sent military advisors. But troops soon followed. Eventually U.S. forces supplied the majority of soldiers, weapons, and equipment used for fighting in the South.

The United States had one of the strongest military forces in the world. U.S. weapons, vehicles, and gear outmatched North Vietnam's military. The United States and its allies believed the North Vietnamese Army and the Viet Cong rebels in the South would quickly be defeated.

However, by 1964 a full-scale war was under way. It was unlike anything the United States had ever faced. U.S. soldiers carried a lot of gear and weapons. But Viet Cong fighters carried little equipment. They could launch quick strikes and then disappear into the jungle and local villages. U.S. troops were often unable to tell who the enemy was.

The war dragged on until 1975, when North Vietnamese forces took over South Vietnam's capital city of Saigon. It became one of the longest and costliest wars in U.S. history.

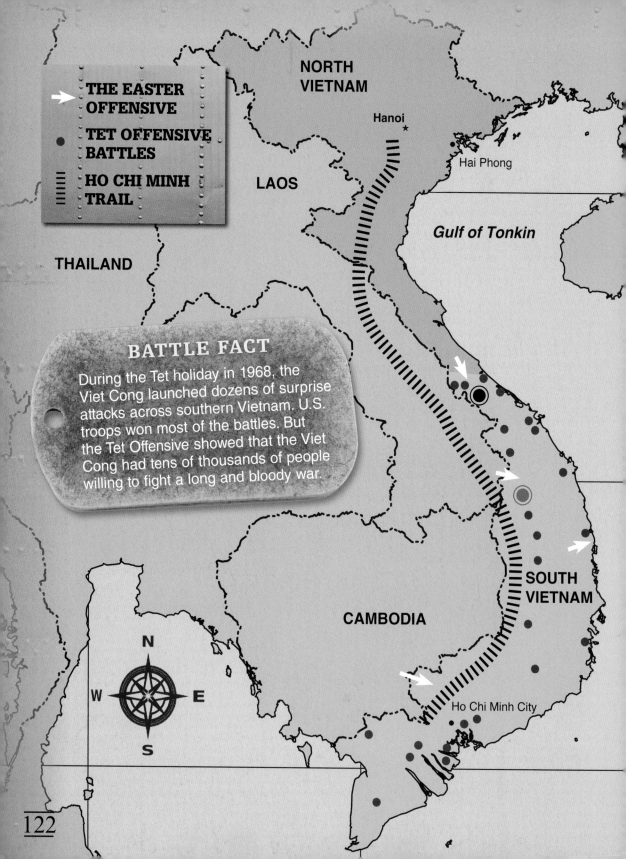

THE EASTER OFFENSIVE

TET OFFENSIVE BATTLES

HO CHI MINH TRAIL

NORTH VIETNAM

Hanoi

Hai Phong

LAOS

Gulf of Tonkin

THAILAND

BATTLE FACT

During the Tet holiday in 1968, the Viet Cong launched dozens of surprise attacks across southern Vietnam. U.S. troops won most of the battles. But the Tet Offensive showed that the Viet Cong had tens of thousands of people willing to fight a long and bloody war.

SOUTH VIETNAM

CAMBODIA

Ho Chi Minh City

N
W   E
S

MAJOR VIETNAM WAR BATTLES

◉ **Battle at Dak To**
Fought: November 3–22, 1967
U.S. and allied casualties: 1,900
North Vietnamese and Viet Cong casualties: 2,600

● **The Tet Offensive**
Fought: January 1–August 30, 1968
U.S. and allied casualties: 45,800
North Vietnamese and Viet Cong casualties: 75,000

◉ **The Siege of Khe Sanh**
Fought: January 21–April 8, 1968
U.S. and allied casualties: 7,400
North Vietnamese and Viet Cong casualties: 10,000–15,000

➔ **The Easter Offensive**
Fought: March 30–October 22, 1972
U.S. and allied casualties: 272,500
North Vietnamese and Viet Cong casualties: 100,000

A TRAIL OF TERROR

The North Vietnamese and the Viet Cong used a secret system of tunnels, small roads, and trails called the Ho Chi Minh Trail. It allowed the fighters to strike fast and hard, and then quickly disappear. The trail also helped them to continually bring in fresh supplies. Some parts of the trail even served as small hospitals or secret weapons factories.

U.S. soldiers sometimes discovered tunnels connected to the trail. Searching the tunnels was dangerous work. Many spots were designed to lure in an enemy soldier who would accidentally set off a booby trap.

NORTH VIETNAMESE ARMY AND VIET CONG UNIFORMS

Vietnam's tropical climate was perfect for the Viet Cong's guerilla warfare. U.S. soldiers struggled in the hot, rainy conditions. But the Viet Cong were used to the heat of the jungle and used it to their advantage. Vietnamese soldiers wore a variety of uniforms, depending on their position with the North Vietnamese Army.

OFFICIAL ARMY HELMETS

North Vietnamese soldiers wore helmets made of pressed paper. Helmets sometimes included the army's five-pointed star symbol on the front.

OFFICIAL ARMY UNIFORMS

Official North Vietnamese soldiers wore green canvas shirts and pants.

VIET CONG HEADGEAR

Viet Cong fighters usually wore floppy cotton hats or cone-shaped wicker hats. A few fighters wore simple plastic helmets that were covered with rubber.

BATTLE FACT

Vietnam has a long season of heavy rain called a monsoon. Parts of the country get more than 100 inches (254 cm) of rain a year. The wet, swampy countryside was difficult to march through and fight in.

VIET CONG UNIFORMS

The Viet Cong needed to quickly blend into local villages. They wore black cotton shirts and pants. Sometimes they wore canvas pants like local farmers. American soldiers never knew if a villager was friend or foe.

VIET CONG FOOTWEAR

The Viet Cong wore sandals like regular villagers. The sandals were often made from recycled tires.

U.S. UNIFORMS

Rain ponchos and jungle boots were as important for U.S. soldiers as guns and grenades. The U.S. military worked hard to provide soldiers with uniforms suitable for jungle warfare. They spent large amounts of money to create special gear such as boots designed to reduce blisters and jungle rot.

AIR FORCE LEATHER COMBAT BOOTS

If a U.S. airplane or helicopter was shot down, sometimes fires broke out in the cockpit. Pilots wore special boots designed to resist burning in case of a fire.

U.S. MILITARY JUNGLE BOOTS

Jungle boots were designed with steel-reinforced insoles to help protect soldiers against spiked booby traps. The boots were also specially designed to drain away water and provide good air movement.

JUNGLE HELMETS

Helmets helped protect soldiers' heads, but they were hot and heavy. Some soldiers liked to keep nets on their helmets. They could pull the nets down to keep mosquitoes from biting their necks and faces.

COMBAT JACKETS

Combat jackets were lightweight and quick to dry. They were well-suited for the jungles of Vietnam. But the buttons often got caught on weeds and branches.

BATTLE FACT

Rats were a terrible problem for soldiers. At night, dozens of large rats would scamper into camp to search for food.

U.S. GEAR

U.S. soldiers could be away from their base for weeks at a time. In addition to their weapons, they had to carry a lot of heavy gear. Much of their gear was designed to help them survive in the jungle.

HEAVY-DUTY PONCHOS

Rubber ponchos were heavy, hot, and uncomfortable. Soldiers complained that it was easier to sit in the rain than to sweat under a poncho. However, ponchos did provide protection against mosquitoes, fire ants, roaches, and scorpions.

WATER PURIFICATION TABLETS

Soldiers carried water purification tablets for their drinking water. Drinking untreated water could lead to serious diseases.

ANTI-PERSONNEL MINES

Anti-personnel mines were used to form a protective barrier around soldiers' night camps. If triggered, a mine shot 700 steel balls across a 150-foot (45-m) wide area. This gave soldiers some protection from nighttime attacks.

MINE DETECTORS

Soldiers used mine detectors to locate mines and other hidden weapons in Vietnamese villages. Land mines were a common weapon of the Viet Cong.

PRC-25 RADIOS

These radios were widely used in the war. Soldiers used the radios to stay in contact with other soldiers on the battlefield. The battery lasted up to 20 hours.

NORTH VIETNAMESE AND VIET CONG GEAR

The North Vietnamese Army and the Viet Cong were not as well supplied as U.S. forces. They had a shortage of radios and often had to carry messages on foot. Soldiers had to travel light so they could move quickly along the Ho Chi Minh Trail.

VIET CONG SURVIVAL KITS

The Viet Cong carried survival kits. The kits usually included medicinal herbs and spices, tea, bandages, and syringes.

ENVIRONMENTAL DISGUISES

The North Vietnamese were experts at blending into their surroundings. They carried a circular frame on their backs with grass and brush attached to it. When helicopters or planes flew overhead, the soldiers lay flat on the ground to hide.

MESS KITS

North Vietnamese mess kits included a bowl, chopsticks, a spoon, and a tube of dried rice. Most soldiers ate rice every day.

BATTLE FACT

The Viet Cong dug up and reused land mines and unexploded bombs from previous conflicts. They used the parts to make new mines and weapons. Making these low-tech bombs was dangerous work. Many died while building the explosives.

ALL-PURPOSE CANVAS BAGS

Viet Cong fighters carried a canvas bag filled with rice and little else. They didn't want to weigh themselves down with a lot of supplies. They liked to enter the Ho Chi Minh Trail to get their supplies instead. They often stopped in villages to demand food from villagers as well.

HAMMOCKS

A hammock provided more comfort than sleeping on the ground. It also offered North Vietnamese soldiers protection from rats, snakes, and other creatures that were active at night. Sometimes soldiers hung their hammocks in old, damaged buildings for shelter.

RUCKSACKS

North Vietnamese soldiers carried food rations, first-aid kits, and other important items in rucksacks.

NORTH VIETNAMESE AND VIET CONG LIGHT WEAPONS

Soldiers from both sides carried lightweight weapons and explosives. Many of the North Vietnamese Army's weapons were old guns from the Soviet Union and China. Viet Cong fighters often made their own lightweight weapons.

AK-47 RIFLES

North Vietnamese soldiers used mainly AK-47 rifles. These rifles were lightweight. They fired ammunition from a big clip and loaded quickly.

HANDMADE WEAPONS

When weapons were hard to come by, the Viet Cong made their own. They used bike parts and pieces of old guns to craft handmade rifles. Sometimes water pipes were fashioned into homemade shotguns. Although crude, these weapons were still deadly.

SKS CARBINES

Developed by the Soviet Union, the SKS Carbine was a 7.62 mm semi-automatic gun. It had a folding bayonet attached to the underside of the barrel. Soldiers could load bullets manually. Or they could fire ammunition automatically from a 10-round clip.

75 MM RECOILLESS RIFLES

China supplied Vietnam with large 75 mm recoilless rifles. The guns could be mounted on wheeled carriages, which made them into small artillery pieces. A direct hit from one of these guns could destroy a bunker.

U.S. LIGHT WEAPONS

After World War II (1939–1945), the U.S. military continued improving its weapons. The government developed new weapons to prepare for potential war with the Soviet Union. Many of the new weapons were used during the conflict in Vietnam.

M16 RIFLES

U.S. soldiers began using the lightweight M16 rifle in Vietnam. It replaced the M14, which tended to jam. It weighed just 7 pounds (3 kg), and its ammunition was lighter than the M14's.

12-GAUGE SHOTGUNS

U.S. soldiers often used 12-gauge shotguns when fighting enemies at close range. The gun's wide blast made it a useful weapon against Viet Cong raids.

M9A1-7 FLAMETHROWERS

Flamethrowers helped U.S. soldiers when searching underground tunnels. They could blast a flame through a tunnel to clear it of enemies. Flamethrowers were also useful in ground battles. Soldiers set fire to trees and dry plants on the ground, forcing the enemy to retreat.

M60 MACHINE GUNS

The M60 was a heavy machine gun. At 23 pounds (10 kg), soldiers called it "the pig." One soldier fired the gun while a second soldier fed it with an ammunition belt. The M60 could fire 550 rounds per minute.

BLADES, GRENADES, AND BOOBY TRAPS

Both the U.S. and North Vietnamese armies used various blades and small explosives. Grenades were a key weapon for U.S. soldiers. Bayonets served well as weapons for soldiers on guard duty. And the Viet Cong created many types of booby traps that took enemy troops by surprise.

M7 BAYONETS

U.S. soldiers often used the M7 bayonet as a general-purpose knife. It was lightweight and useful in hand-to-hand combat. It could be attached to an M16 rifle to use as a thrusting weapon during a charge attack.

GRENADES

Both the U.S. military and the Viet Cong used grenades heavily during the war. The Viet Cong often used them in booby traps. They sometimes attached a grenade to a bamboo spike in a pit trap. If a victim was pulled out of the pit, the grenade exploded to injure or kill several more men. The Viet Cong also attached trip wires to grenades. The grenades would explode as enemy troops marched through the jungle.

LAND MINES

The Viet Cong buried tens of thousands of land mines across the country. When a soldier stepped on the mine and lifted his foot, the mine would explode. The Viet Cong often got villagers to gather pieces of exploded land mines to rebuild and reuse them.

CLUSTER BOMBS

The United States used millions of cluster bombs during the war. Cluster bombs could be dropped from airplanes or launched with rockets. They held several "mini-bombs" that were about the size of tennis balls. When fired, a canister would open in midair and widely scatter the mini-bombs over the enemy.

PUNJI SPIKE BOOBY TRAPS

Punji spikes made terrifying weapons. The Viet Cong often placed these bamboo spikes in a pit, then covered the pit with branches and leaves to hide it. When an enemy fell in the trap, he would be stabbed with the spikes. The spikes were usually smeared with poison or human waste to make the wounds more deadly.

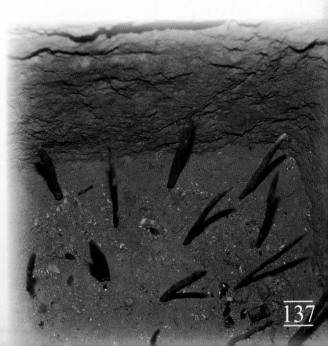

ARTILLERY

Soldiers used heavy weapons and artillery to support troops in battle. The weapons could be fired from base camps or they could be moved into the field. Soldiers counted on the large guns to destroy the enemy's artillery and break up large groups of enemy fighters.

105 MM HOWITZERS

The 105 mm howitzer was a huge gun used by the U.S. military. It had to be towed into the battlefield. It took eight men to operate the gun, which could fire up to eight rounds per minute.

M19 60 MM MORTARS

The M19 60 mm mortar was a small field support weapon. It could be carried by a single U.S. soldier. It shot up to 30 explosives per minute.

SA7 GRAIL ANTI-AIRCRAFT MISSILES

Low-flying U.S. planes and helicopters were under constant threat by SA7 Grail anti-aircraft missiles. The Soviet-made weapon used a heat-seeking guidance system and carried a 2.5-pound (1.1-kg) warhead.

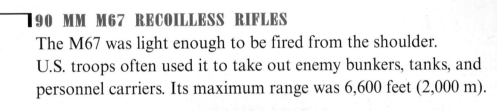

90 MM M67 RECOILLESS RIFLES

The M67 was light enough to be fired from the shoulder. U.S. troops often used it to take out enemy bunkers, tanks, and personnel carriers. Its maximum range was 6,600 feet (2,000 m).

M46 130 MM FIELD GUNS

This field gun was a key artillery piece for the North Vietnamese. The Soviet-designed gun fired a 74-pound (34-kg) shell nearly 17 miles (27 km).

ARMORED VEHICLES

Tanks and jeeps did not perform well in the wettest areas of Vietnam. They often got stuck in the mud. But in spite of the wet climate, both U.S. and North Vietnamese forces fought with a variety of armored vehicles during the war.

M48 TANKS

In southern Vietnam, U.S. soldiers used the M48 tank to secure and control roads. It traveled about 30 miles (48 km) per hour and carried two machine guns.

BATTLE FACT

The Viet Cong occasionally traveled and hauled equipment with elephants.

M-113 ARMORED PERSONNEL CARRIERS

When the U.S. military transported soldiers through dangerous areas, they often used M-113 armored personnel carriers. These vehicles held up to 11 soldiers and traveled at 40 miles (64 km) per hour. The M-113 also served as an anti-aircraft and flamethrower vehicle.

BMP-1 ARMORED PERSONNEL CARRIERS

North Vietnamese soldiers used the BMP-1. This armored personnel carrier was designed and produced by the Soviet Union. It was first used in World War II. It could move over land and through water.

HELICOPTERS AND PLANES

The conflict in Vietnam saw the first heavy use of helicopters in combat. There were few places for airplanes to land in Vietnam's thick jungles. But helicopters could land in small clearings to drop off and pick up soldiers.

BELL UH-1

The Bell UH-1, nicknamed the "Huey," was a good fit for jungle warfare. It could land in small clearings. It was often used to pick up wounded or dead soldiers. It was also used to quickly drop off troops who could attack with little warning.

MIG-21 FIGHTERS

Soviet-built MiG-21s were the primary fighter planes for the North Vietnamese. These fast flyers were armed with air-to-air missiles. The North Vietnamese often used these planes to disrupt U.S. bombing missions.

CH-54 TARHE

The CH-54 Tarhe was a new kind of helicopter. It was a real workhorse for the United States. It could carry a load of up to 20,000 pounds (9,072 kg). It often carried heavy equipment to bases for repair.

B-52 STRATOFORTRESS BOMBERS

The huge B-52 Stratofortress bomber could carry up to 60,000 pounds (27,215 kg) of bombs at one time. Its huge payload helped break up the Viet Cong's supply lines. U.S. pilots flew 124,532 missions with the B-52 in Vietnam.

F-4 PHANTOM II

The North Vietnamese gave U.S. ground forces a hard time with the MiG-21. But U.S. forces had the F-4 Phantom II. This fighter plane was faster. And it carried a variety of weapons, including radar-guided bombs.

SHIPS AND RIVER BOATS

Vietnam was mainly a jungle war, but the U.S. Navy also had a role. Aircraft carriers supported air strikes, while naval ships provided seaside gunfire. However, Vietnam's rivers played a more important role in the war. The Viet Cong used the rivers as supply routes. To stop them, the U.S. Navy created a "Brown Water Navy" that patrolled the rivers.

RIVER PATROL BOATS

River patrol boats stopped shipments of weapons and supplies in Vietnam's rivers. They were sleek, fast boats that carried machine guns, grenade launchers, and cannons.

ALPHA BOATS

U.S. Alpha boats were designed to withstand blasts from underwater mines. Their job was to sweep the river before the patrol boats arrived.

JUNKS

North Vietnamese forces used small, sleek boats called "junks." They weren't designed to be used in battle. Instead, they were used to sneak weapons and supplies to troops on the rivers.

CHEMICAL WEAPONS

Vietnam's thick jungle provided cover for the Viet Cong. To overcome this, U.S. forces dropped napalm on enemy positions. Napalm is a chemical substance that burns hotter than 2,000 degrees Fahrenheit (1,093 degrees Celsius). The thick, sticky chemical clung to people's skin and caused severe burns. Most victims died.

U.S. forces also used chemicals to strip the leaves off trees and plants. The chemicals had code names like Agent Orange and Agent Purple. However, the chemicals hurt more than just plants. People exposed to the chemicals often became sick. Children were often born with severe birth defects. U.S. soldiers suffered bad effects from the chemicals too. Many became sick after they returned home.

EQUIPPED FOR BATTLE

WEAPONS, GEAR, AND UNIFORMS

❖ OF THE ❖

IRAQ WAR

⟡THE IRAQ WAR⟡

In 1991 the United States and its allies defeated the Iraqi Army in a fast and furious battle. The source of the conflict was Iraq's invasion of its small neighbor Kuwait. After months of threats and troop movements, the U.S.-led nations won Operation Desert Storm in just four days. Iraqi leader Saddam Hussein was forced to pull his forces back to Iraq.

But the seeds of war soon began growing again. Hussein had always been interested in gas, biological, and nuclear weapons. He had used such weapons of mass destruction (WMDs) in previous conflicts. After the 1991 war, United Nations weapons inspectors had tried to search Iraq for WMDs. But Hussein continually resisted the inspections. Many world leaders believed Hussein was secretly developing WMDs. By the end of 2002, the United States began calling for another attack on Iraq.

In March 2003, the United States and its allies launched Operation Iraqi Freedom. Hussein's forces were quickly crushed. It looked like it would be another easy victory. U.S. and allied forces stayed in Iraq to provide support as a new government was formed. But many Iraqis did not like the new government. Insurgents rose up to fight against it. The allies soon found themselves in a long conflict that would drag on for years.

MAJOR COMBAT

 DAY 1: MARCH 20, 2003
- Baghdad is hit with 40 Tomahawk cruise missiles.
- U.S. F-117 Stealth fighter planes drop bombs guided by satellites into Baghdad.
- Iraq sends missiles into Kuwait, but they are intercepted by U.S. Patriot missiles.

 DAY 6: MARCH 25, 2003
- The U.S. Army approaches Karbala near Baghdad.

● **DAY 12: MARCH 31, 2003**
- Baghdad is repeatedly bombed.
- British forces prepare to attack Basra, which is still defended by Iraqi troops.

● **DAY 18: APRIL 6, 2003**
- 2,000 to 3,000 Iraqi troops are killed in southern Baghdad.
- British forces continue marching toward Basra.

● **DAY 27: APRIL 15, 2003**
- Iraq's new leaders gather to create a new government.

● **DAY 43: MAY 1, 2003**
- U.S. President George W. Bush announces the end of major combat in Iraq.

N W E S

SYRIA

INVASION OF IRAQ, 2003

IRAQ

U.S. TROOP MOVEMENT

BRITISH TROOP MOVEMENT

Baghdad ★

Karbala

Basra

BATTLE FACT

Saddam Hussein was captured on December 13, 2003. U.S. forces found him hiding in an underground hideout at a farm near Tikrit, Iraq. He was found guilty of crimes against humanity and sentenced to death.

KUWAIT

U.S. UNIFORMS

In times of war, soldiers need a variety of reliable weapons, clothing, and gear. In Iraq the weather can be extreme. During the war, violent sandstorms swirled in temperatures reaching 120 degrees Fahrenheit (49 degrees Celsius) or more. But in spite of the heat, U.S. soldiers had to wear heavy uniforms to protect them from burns, bugs, and bullets.

FLAME-RESISTANT UNIFORMS

Soldiers often risked coming into contact with roadside bombs. To reduce injuries, they wore flame-retardant suits. The material resisted burning for about nine seconds—long enough to jump from a burning vehicle.

COMBAT HELMETS

Padded helmets reduced brain injuries. A face shield was sometimes attached to the helmet to prevent injuries to the face.

DESERT BOOTS

Desert boots had heat-resistant soles. Vents on the boots were eliminated to keep sand and dirt out. Moisture-wicking inserts helped keep soldiers' feet cool and dry.

U.S. STANDARD UNIFORMS

U.S. soldiers wore camouflage uniforms with a combination of gray, light green, and tan. The colors allowed soldiers to blend in with inner-city and desert environments.

BATTLE FACT

Soldiers had to closely inspect their boots before putting them on. During the evening, small snakes, scorpions, or poisonous spiders sometimes made their homes inside boots.

IRAQI UNIFORMS

Most Iraqi forces wore standard camouflage clothing. But Saddam Hussein's best troops wore uniforms that set them apart from other soldiers. Meanwhile, insurgent fighters could be anyone, anywhere. They often looked like normal Iraqi citizens.

IRAQI REPUBLICAN GUARD UNIFORMS

The Iraqi Republican Guard were the best soldiers of the Iraqi military. Their uniforms included olive green shirts, jackets, and pants. Members of the guard also wore a red triangle insignia on their sleeves.

FEDAYEEN MILITIA

Saddam Hussein's special forces unit was called the Fedayeen Militia. These fighters wore all black uniforms and continued fighting after the regular military had surrendered.

CEREMONIAL CAPS

An olive green cap was worn by members of the military during ceremonial duties. The hat featured the country's national symbol—a bird bordered with blue stars.

IRAQI HELMETS

Iraqi troops wore combat helmets that looked similar to U.S. helmets from World War II (1939–1945). However, the helmets were made from fiberglass and plastic. They offered little protection against bullets.

INSURGENTS

Insurgent fighters wore regular clothes to avoid calling attention to themselves. To disguise themselves, many wore kaffiyehs over their faces.

U.S. GEAR

Heat and dust created uncomfortable conditions for soldiers in the desert. The environment was also hard on the troops' gear. The temperatures and sand caused gear to break down. The equipment needed constant repair and replacement.

NIGHT-VISION GOGGLES

Night-vision goggles magnify light from stars and the moon. Pilots used them to see mountains and other obstacles while flying at night in the desert. Ground troops also used night-vision scopes for nighttime missions.

BODY ARMOR

Body armor was made of ceramic plates strong enough to stop bullets and shrapnel. But it was also hot and heavy. Many soldiers took off their armor to prevent heat stroke.

BATTLE FACT
Body armor weighed up to 60 pounds (27 kg). Some soldiers said the extra weight kept them from catching quick-footed insurgents.

MODULAR LIGHTWEIGHT LOAD-CARRYING EQUIPMENT

This vest held a variety of equipment, including ammunition, grenades, a radio, batteries, and knives. It also included a special suit to protect against chemical and biological attacks.

PROTECTIVE SUNGLASSES

Sunglasses and goggles protected soldiers' eyes from bright sunlight. They also had special foam seals to keep out dust and sand.

THE LAND WARRIOR

The Land Warrior was a mobile computer module attached to a soldier's helmet. It allowed the soldier to track locations, view maps, and review battle plans. Military leaders could send e-mails or talk to anyone wearing the system.

IRAQI AND INSURGENT GEAR

U.S. forces quickly defeated the official Iraqi military at the beginning of the war. However, insurgent fighters soon began causing problems. Insurgents often used gear and weapons left behind by Iraq's military. They also used farm equipment, tools, and other everyday items to create useful weapons and gear.

BANDOLEERS

Iraqi soldiers often wore bandoleers. A soldier would wear one or two of these cotton belts across his chest and shoulders. The bandoleer carried clips of ammunition used for the soldier's gun.

INSURGENT ADAPTATIONS

Insurgents sometimes turned low-tech objects into useful equipment. Homemade rocket launchers and other weapons could be made from everyday objects such as pipes and duct tape.

RECORDING DEVICES

Insurgents didn't have official methods of communication. They carried cameras and video recorders to document their missions instead. They published the images on the Internet to try to scare people and motivate their followers.

BATTLE FACT

Early in the war, the U.S. military did not have enough body armor or helmets for all the soldiers. Family members often bought these items and shipped them to U.S. bases.

RUNNING SHOES

Insurgent fighters and snipers usually wore lightweight running shoes instead of heavy boots. Running shoes allowed them to attack quickly and then run away. They were constantly on the move to keep from getting caught.

U.S. LIGHT WEAPONS

U.S. troops used a variety of light weapons to shoot over short distances and fight in close combat. In the desert environment, light weapons needed to be carefully cleaned and cared for. Some high-tech weapons were sensitive to tiny grains of damaging sand.

M-4 ASSAULT RIFLES

The M-4 weighed about 6 pounds (2.7 kg) and used a 30-round magazine. It was a very reliable weapon as long as it was kept clean and well-maintained.

LIGHTWEIGHT SHOTGUNS

Soldiers often used lightweight shotguns to help break through doors. These guns were also known as XM-26 Modular Accessory Shotgun Systems.

M1911-A2 PISTOLS

The original M1911 was a very successful design that was first used in World War I (1914–1918). Updated versions were used in Iraq by both regular troops and special forces.

M249 SQUAD AUTOMATIC WEAPONS

The M249 was a portable gas-operated machine gun. It was used to support infantry troops. It could hit targets at ranges of up to 2,625 feet (800 m).

M24 SNIPER WEAPON SYSTEMS

Snipers needed to pass special training to use this rifle. Shooters were trained to hit targets from 325 to 2,600 feet (100 to 800 m) away using this system. The weapon used armor-piercing ammunition.

IRAQI AND INSURGENT LIGHT WEAPONS

The traditional Iraqi army was well supplied. However, insurgent fighters had to steal weapons or buy them illegally. Some countries that supported the insurgency also supplied weapons. Insurgents sometimes fixed old weapons and land mines to make them useable again.

PKM MACHINE GUNS

The PKM was a Soviet-made weapon. Its ammunition was held in a detachable barrel. It had dust covers over the loading and ejection windows to keep sand out of the weapon.

ROCK THROWING

Insurgents knew that U.S. soldiers would not fire at children. They convinced mobs of young boys to throw rocks at U.S. soldiers. The U.S. troops could be injured if they didn't duck out of the way.

RECYCLED LAND MINES

In the 1980s Iraq was involved in a long war against Iran. During the conflict, Iraqi forces buried millions of land mines throughout the country. Insurgents often dug up these old land mines, repaired them, and used them against U.S. and allied troops.

AKM RIFLES

The Soviet AKM replaced the AK-47 assault rifle of the late 1940s. It was lighter, cheaper, and easier for a soldier to control. It is considered one of the most successful firearms ever produced.

EXPLOSIVES

Explosives are a key part of modern warfare. U.S. forces often used weapons that launched explosives at the enemy. Meanwhile, the insurgents thought of new ways to use explosives. They often littered roads with improvised explosive devices, or IEDs.

U.S. M32 MULTIPLE-SHOT GRENADE LAUNCHERS

The M32 could quickly shoot many grenades with a high degree of accuracy. Quickly firing several grenades was an improvement over single-shot launchers.

IMPROVISED EXPLOSIVE DEVICES (IEDS)

IEDs were made from mortar and artillery pieces. Insurgents often threw these at vehicles or buried them on roads to explode as vehicles traveled over them. Some IEDs could be detonated by a remote control or a cell phone.

U.S. AT-4 ANTI-TANK MISSILE LAUNCHERS

The AT-4 launched guided missiles through a tube. Missiles traveled 600 feet (183 m) per second. They had a maximum range of 6,560 feet (2,000 m). A three-man team was required to carry and set up the weapon. One soldier carried the launcher and tripod while the other two carried the launch tubes.

VEHICLE-BORNE IMPROVISED EXPLOSIVE DEVICES

Insurgents placed some IEDs inside vehicles. These bombs contained explosive charges ranging from 100 to 1,000 pounds (45 to 454 kg). Insurgents often drove these vehicle-based bombs into crowded areas to kill as many people as possible.

SUICIDE BOMB IMPROVISED EXPLOSIVE DEVICES

Some insurgents hid explosive devices under their clothing. They entered a large crowd, and then blew themselves up. Their goal was to cause as much death and chaos as possible.

BATTLE FACT

In 2008 women made up 11 percent of the military units in Iraq and Afghanistan. According to CNN, 180,000 women were in the war zone at that time.

MISSILES AND SMART BOMBS

Heavy weapons range from large guns to cruise missiles and vehicles. These deadly weapons were used to take out enemy positions and send enemy troops on the run. Some large weapons were fired from military bases, while others had to be transported to battle sites.

U.S. M777 HOWITZERS

The M777 could be quickly delivered to the battlefield by a helicopter. It had an onboard computer that helped it fire rounds at targets up to 19 miles (31 km) away.

U.S. PATRIOT MISSILE DEFENSE SYSTEMS

Stationed far from battle, the Patriot missile system tracked incoming enemy missiles. A computer guided Patriot missiles toward enemy missiles to shoot them down. However, the Patriot system wasn't always very accurate at hitting incoming missiles.

IRAQI SCUD MISSILES

Iraq had a supply of old Soviet SCUD missiles. The Iraqi military adapted the missiles to fly over longer distances. They also armed the missiles with chemical and biological weapons.

U.S. TOMAHAWK CRUISE MISSILES

Tomahawk missiles could be launched from ships or submarines. They were hard to trace with radar. Tomahawks could hit targets up to 1,550 miles (2,500 km) away.

AIRCRAFT

The United States had an edge in the air war over Iraq. With a bigger budget and better technology, U.S. forces ruled the skies. The United States also improved its ability to target specific military locations and reduce the number of civilian deaths.

U.S. B-2 SPIRIT STEALTH BOMBERS

B-2 Spirit bombers carried up to 40,000 pounds (18,000 kg) of weapons. They also carried an advanced cruise missile with a range of up to 1,500 miles (2,414 km).

F-117 NIGHTHAWK STEALTH FIGHTERS

F-117 Nighthawk stealth fighters were officially retired in 2008. The plane allowed pilots to receive new information and redirect a mission from the cockpit. Its advanced attack systems helped U.S. forces fly many successful missions. No Nighthawks were lost in combat during the war.

AH-1W SUPER COBRA ATTACK HELICOPTERS

The Super Cobra was based on the original Huey helicopter that was used in the Vietnam War (1959–1975). Its twin-engine design made it more stable and safer for pilots.

BATTLE FACT

Specially trained dolphins helped the U.S. Navy clear mines near the port city of Umm Qasr.

U.S. A-10 WARTHOG JETS

The A-10 Warthogs were key weapons in the war's first days. They disrupted and destroyed Saddam Hussein's fleet of tanks. The jets could fly low to support ground troops and hunt down enemy vehicles.

TANKS AND ASSAULT VEHICLES

The United States had more tanks and assault vehicles than Iraq. The vehicles were also more advanced. The Iraqi forces used older tanks from China and the former Soviet Union. Insurgent fighters sometimes used buses and trucks as combat vehicles.

T-72 SOVIET TANKS

Originally designed by the Soviets, the T-72s were the best tanks in the Iraqi military. They were used by the Republican Guard. Regular forces used lesser quality tanks, such as the Chinese-built T-55.

U.S. M2 BRADLEY FIGHTING VEHICLES

The M2 Bradley was designed to carry troops into battle. It was one of the U.S. military's most heavily armored vehicles in the war. It protected soldiers from bullets and explosives.

U.S. LAND ROVERS

Land Rovers were non-military vehicles that were modified for use as light utility vehicles. They could also carry and fire anti-tank weapons. Armor was added to protect the driver and passengers.

U.S. ARMORED HUMVEES

Humvees were one of the U.S. army's main transport vehicles. Up-armored Humvees were fitted with special kits that included armored doors and body panels and bullet-proof glass. The armor helped protect soldiers from enemy fire and IEDs.

MINE RESISTANT AMBUSH PROTECTED VEHICLES (MRAPS)

MRAPs were designed to deflect a blast away from the vehicle when it hit a roadside bomb. It was believed that survival rates were four to five times greater than with armored Humvees.

Every war brings new challenges. New technology is often created to meet those challenges. During the Vietnam War, helicopters became the superstars of the skies. In the Iraq War, computers and other inventions helped protect U.S. troops and defeat the enemy.

THERMAL IMAGING DEVICES

In past wars, soldiers used binoculars to see distant enemies. In Iraq they often used thermal imaging. This technology allowed soldiers to clearly see what the enemy was doing several miles away—even through darkness and fog.

GLOBAL POSITIONING SYSTEM (GPS)

American drivers often use GPS technology to avoid getting lost on the road. These systems were greatly improved during the Iraq War. U.S. troops could use a GPS with an accuracy range of 10 feet (3 m).

SATELLITE JAMMERS

Iraqi insurgents used low-cost satellite jammers to interfere with U.S. troops' GPS units. However, U.S. forces soon developed anti-jamming technology.

UNMANNED AERIAL VEHICLES (UAVS)

Unmanned aerial vehicles weren't new during the Iraq War. But advancements made them lighter and more effective than before. The vehicles could be tucked into a soldier's backpack and pulled out when needed.

FORCE XXI BATTLE COMMAND BRIGADE-AND-BELOW (FBCB2)

U.S. commanders used the FBCB2 system to track enemies on the battlefield. They could share the enemy's locations with their troops during battles. This advanced computer system took the guesswork out of how, when, and where to fight.

INDEX